D1123727

Crosse, Jesse.
The greatest movie car
chases of all time /
c2006.
33305212494672
mi   10/16/07

THE GREATEST
MOVIE
CAR
CHASES
OF ALL TIME

JESSE CROSSE

MOTORBOOKS

To Wendy, Zoe, and Alex

First published in 2006 by Motorbooks, an imprint of MBI Publishing Company, Galtier Plaza, Suite 200, 380 Jackson Street, St. Paul, MN 55101-3885 USA.

Copyright © 2006 by Jesse Crosse

All rights reserved. With the exception of quoting brief passages for the purposes of review, no part of this publication may be reproduced without prior written permission from the Publisher.

The information in this book is true and complete to the best of our knowledge. All recommendations are made without any guarantee on the part of the author or Publisher, who also disclaim any liability incurred in connection with the use of this data or specific details.

We recognize, further, that some words, model names, and designations mentioned herein are the property of the trademark holder. We use them for identification purposes only. This is not an official publication.

MBI Publishing Company titles are also available at discounts in bulk quantity for industrial or sales-promotional use. For details write to Special Sales Manager at MBI Publishing Company, Galtier Plaza, Suite 200, 380 Jackson Street, St. Paul, MN 55101-3885 USA

ISBN-13: 978-0-7603-2410-3
ISBN-10: 0-7603-2410-7

Editor: Scott Pearson
Designer: Sara Grindle

Printed in China

On the front cover: Stunt driver Bill Hickman's Charger R/T, the bad guy to Steve McQueen's righteous Mustang in *Bullitt. Solar Productions/Warner Bros/RGA*

On the endpapers: Action! Four decades of car chases. See individual pictures in the book for complete photo credits.

On the frontispiece: Always cool Steve McQueen at the wheel of his *Bullitt* Mustang. S*olar Productions/Warner Bros/RGA*

On the title page: The ghostly Twins of *The Matrix Reloaded* momentarily set aside martial arts for a shoot-'em-up car chase. *General Motors*

On the back cover: *Keystone Kops*: in the beginning . . . *Keystone Film Co./RGA*
The Blues Brothers: cop motors, cop tires, cop suspensions, cop shocks. *Universal/RGA*
The French Connection: the famous chase, car vs. el train. *20th Century Fox/RGA*
The Road Warrior: post-apocalyptic road rage. *Kennedy Miller Productions/RGA*
The Rock: even cable cars blow up good, real good. *Don Simpson/Jerry Bruckheimer Films/Hollywood Pictures/RGA*

CONTENTS

FOREWORD
BY PETER YATES

At last, what seems to me to be the definitive guide to—and analysis of—car chases on film! I have found Jesse Crosse's wonderfully documented research both entertaining and educational. Anyone fascinated by (or even interested in) the history of the car in film cannot fail to be riveted by this book. It has been a delight for me to read the details of so many famous chases. The earliest chases documented are those of the Keystone Kops, Buster Keaton, and Harold Lloyd—no stunt doubles or digital enhancement were available in the early twentieth century, but we can still learn from the wonderful sequences filmed by the pioneers.

For true car buffs, the detailed accounts of some of the cinema's most famous chases will prove endlessly intriguing: the backgrounds, the necessary modifications of machinery, and the inevitable problems. One always tries to make a chase sequence appear completely spontaneous, but this is far from the reality of the actual filming. The preparation is complicated and demanding—involving all the departments of the film unit itself and the cooperation of the police and other local authorities—and finally shooting the sequence is harrowing on every level.

I am flattered to have been asked to write a foreword to this book which pays tribute to so many of the talents who have contributed to this special medium.

London
10 October 2005

Right: **Peter Yates during the filming of *The Deep* (1977). He's wearing an F+B Ambulance Service cap, the name of the ambulance company from *Mother, Jugs & Speed* (1976). *Peter Yates***

PREFACE
THE RUSHES

What is it about movie car chases that makes them so compelling? Do they only appeal to car nuts, or do they promise the kind of action that appeals to anyone, male or female, young or old? Do we wish we were the ones behind the wheel, or are we simply relieved to be watching someone else risk their neck? Maybe it's just the fast film editing, the scream of tortured engines, and the wail of burning tire rubber . . . who knows? Whatever the psychology, one thing's for sure: car chases have not only kept us glued to our seats through generations of filmmaking, but some have even become the stuff of legend. A relatively short sequence of film—often thought of by the filmmakers as a low-priority component of the story during production—has sometimes become *the* scene that defines a movie and lingers in a viewer's memory for years.

In writing this book, I was amazed and also horrified to discover just how many scenes there are in dozens of movies that constitute a car chase. Whenever I'd meet up with a fellow journalist somewhere and mention this project over a beer, chances were it would unleash a barrage of great chase scenes that I absolutely *had to* see. The enthusiastic response I always got made me realize just how popular car chases are and how insatiable our desire is to see more. But at the same time I eventually became so overloaded with suggestions, I realized it would be safer to button my lip. The main problem I had, though, was how to sort the wheat from the chaff and decide exactly what constituted a "proper" car chase. I didn't want my Top Twenty to become just another list of random stunt sequences involving cars. I wasn't going to include road movies such as *Two-Lane Blacktop* or *Thelma & Louise*. I also wasn't going to consider great racing movies such as *Grand Prix*, *Le Mans,* or, to stretch a point, *The Gumball Rally* or *Cannonball Run*.

To me a car chase is a pursuit scene that has its own beginning and end within the movie; Jake and Elwood careening through the shopping mall in *The Blues Brothers*, for example. That example aside, the very best have at least a hint of serious intent; to be really gripped by the action you have to believe that this is a life-or-death moment for those taking part, and it must be real enough to flood your veins with adrenalin, make the hairs stand up on the back of your neck, and leave you with a tangible sense of relief when it's over. That's not always the case of course—sometimes it's possible to kick back, have a laugh, and just enjoy the humor and the brilliance of the filmmaking. There are contradictions too, like *Vanishing Point*. Is it a road movie or a series of car chases? I think the latter, so it's in. Perhaps the only real indulgence is the inclusion of *C'était un Rendezvous* (literally, "It was an appointment") by Claude

Lelouch. OK, there are no police cars actually chasing the mystery Ferrari on its mission against the clock through Paris, but you are convinced there will be at any moment, and it is being pursued by Old Father Time after all.

In attempting to move beyond a mere list, I've talked to lots of people on the sharp end of filmmaking while writing this book. They all lead fascinating lives filled with practical challenges rather than the esoteric frippery often associated with an industry whose headquarters is unflatteringly known as "Tinseltown." What I've tried to reveal is the anatomy of the great car chases: how they are planned and filmed, the techniques used, and the ingenuity of the equipment makers and special effects people. I became intrigued by the history of the art and discovered a kind of "car chase family." Some people have gained a reputation for creating chases, and their names appear in movie credits time and time again. You can meet them in the first chapter.

Overall, it's been an illuminating journey punctuated by the need to watch some great car chase scenes over and over again. My DVD collection has grown as a result, and I've enjoyed it. I hope you do too.

ACKNOWLEDGMENTS

Thanks to everybody who helped with sourcing information and made time for interviews, most of whom were flat out on various projects at the time. Special thanks to Paul and Dave Bickers at Bickers Action, Vic Armstrong, Michel Cheyko, Remy and Dominique Julienne, Lee Sheward, Jim Dowdall, Andy Smith, Johnny Martin, Harvey Harrison, Barry Dressel at the Walter P. Chrysler Museum, Tom Malcolm (Ford GB), Natalie Wakefield (BMW GB), Tim Watson (Aston Martin), and Martin Humphries at the Ronald Grant Archive for unearthing all the fabulous stills. A huge thanks to the legendary Peter Yates, director of *Bullitt,* for taking the time to read the manuscript and write the foreword. And last but not least, thanks to Rob Golding for liking my idea enough to commission the book and Scott Pearson, my editor at MBI, for his enthusiasm and attention to detail.

CHAPTER 1
DYNASTY

Car chases may appear to be random acts of cinematic fancy. But many have more in common than at first seems obvious—the people who made them.

"Hang on, lads, I've got a great idea."

—*Charlie Croker,* The Italian Job, *1969*

Visit your local megaplex and the chances are there will be at least one film showing in which cars are pipe-rolling into oblivion or otherwise invalidating the manufacturer's warranty in a big way. Gripped by the images before them, car nuts will revel in the driving skills, fantasize their way into the driving seat, and lust after the machinery. Normal people, meanwhile, will feel cozy in the knowledge that automotive horrors they don't even want to think about are happening to a fictitious character on screen instead of to them, and they'll get a kick from it anyway. It's a win-win situation and it's why people have been enjoying on-screen car chase action for years.

Underpinning that enjoyment is a heritage of classic filmmaking traceable back to the 1950s. Intriguingly, many of the best sequences ever made are linked by the people who made them. In fact, far from the car chase evolving in a haphazard way as a series of unrelated stunt scenes in unrelated movies, the finest work has emerged from dynasties of filmmakers who recognized just what a powerful element the car chase could be. Their movement around the industry produced a creative cross-fertilization in which a number of key people were drafted time and again to give a repeat performance. To trace those threads, we'll start by rewinding the tape more than forty years to a film location not in the sun-kissed valleys of Southern California, but in the remote, windswept back roads of Britain. *Hell Drivers*, a little-known 1957 British B-movie, was being shot in black and white. The promotional teaser could have read something like this:

A modern location shoot (a Bond film in this case) has a large crew and plenty of specialized equipment. The roots of car chases, however, go back to a more bare-bones style of filmmaking. *Bickers Action*

Hands sawing desperately at the wheel, sweat pouring from knitted brow, arms aching with fatigue, Tom Yately's weary face is etched by the strain of battling with the heavy 5.5-ton truck for too long. An ex-con trying to go straight and work an honest job, he's unwittingly stumbled upon a scam in which the crooked manager and foreman have created a list of five fictional drivers whose wages are split between the two of them, while the extra shifts are shouldered by the existing wheelmen. They can do it, but only just, by driving the evil-handling trucks at impossible speeds.

As Yately's machine bounds and jostles over the rutted track, stretched beyond the limits of its ancient chassis, the director lets us share the full extent of his daring with a sneaked shot of the speedometer's dial. We gasp, grip the arm of the chair, and seek comfort in another handful of popcorn. The spidery needle has just flickered towards a horrific 30 miles per hour. This all seems more than a little tame now, though the plot is engaging enough. It was hardly a car chase movie (no cars), and by today's standards the cumbersome trucks were actually moving at a snail's pace and chasing nothing except the clock. The car chase movie had yet to evolve into the genre it has become—adrenalin-pumping, nail-biting, high-speed action with near misses and not-so-near misses—but *Hell Drivers* sowed seeds of talent for some of the greatest automotive on-screen action the world has ever seen. (It's also a great opportunity to see Sean Connery, Patrick McGoohan, and David McCallum, among others, before they got famous.) The point is that, for its time, the filmmakers had conveyed an involving sense of danger built around reckless, on-the-edge driving.

Stanley Baker as Tom Yately wrestles with the wheel of an ancient British truck in *Hell Drivers*. Baker would go on to form Oakhurst Productions and produce the original *The Italian Job*. Acqua Film Productions/RGA

In *Safety Last*, Harold Lloyd dangles from a fake wall built on a rooftop—providing the real backdrop—and relies on mattresses placed on the roof in case he falls. Lloyd tested the safety of the stunt by dropping a dummy from the wall. The dummy bounced on the mattresses and tumbled over the edge of the building.

Stanley Baker, who played Yately, may well have left the set pondering that subject, because in 1967 he would produce and star in *Robbery*, a film that included the kind of car chase action rarely seen since the early years of the twentieth century. Back then, some of the legendary silent moviemakers had pioneered spectacular action sequences—with or without wheels—that, although dangerous,

Did *The Blues Brothers* find inspiration in the antics of this lot? Probably—and with the Keystone Kops, what we see is what they got! *Keystone Film Co./RGA*

were often played for laughs. The key difference is that whether contemplating Mack Sennett's *Keystone Kops* (1912–1917) surviving numerous automotive disasters, a conveniently placed window saving Buster Keaton from a collapsing wall in *One Week* (1920), or Harold Lloyd dangling from a clock on the side of a building in *Safety Last* (1923), we can be sure that what we see is what they got. Keaton, Lloyd, and the Kops had no choice but to do it for real because there were no stunt doubles, no blue screens, and no computer-generated images (CGI).

Ironically, as film technology improved, the end result often became less convincing, not more so. Sometimes ludicrous back-projection and eventually blue-screen techniques made "faking it" easy, especially with in-car scenes. Realism was frequently sacrificed on the altar of making a scene do-able within the limits of available technology and budget, and *Hell Drivers* had undoubtedly been a culprit. *Thunder Road*, a 1958 Robert Mitchum film about moonshine runners, also relied on studio in-car shots. (Bruce Springsteen—an admitted fan of Mitchum—borrowed the movie's name for "Thunder Road," the first song on his album *Born to Run*. Bringing it full circle on his 2005 solo tour, Springsteen included "The Ballad of Thunder Road," cowritten and sung by Mitchum for the movie, in the recorded music played before the concert: "Let me tell the story, I can tell it all/About the mountain boy who ran illegal alcohol/His daddy made the whiskey, son, he drove the load/When his engine roared, they called the highway Thunder Road.") Thunder Road is a must-see to complete anyone's education on how car chases evolved over the years; the final crash at the end is performed with a savagery that makes you wince. The stunt driver was none other than the legendary Carey Loftin, who later went on to coordinate chases in *Bullitt*, *Vanishing Point*, *The French Connection*, and countless others.

But when *Robbery*, based on the great train robbery of 1963, appeared in 1967, it contained some old-school chase sequences shot in real time with little or no special effects—this time played for danger, not laughs. *Robbery*'s co-producer was Michael Deeley, and the director was thirty-seven-year-old Peter Yates, who had first appeared as assistant director on *Cover Girl Killer* in 1959. But Yates had already accumulated an impressive portfolio, having assisted J. Lee Thompson on *The Guns of Navarone* in 1961 and Tony Richardson on the British classic *A Taste of Honey* in the same year.

Perhaps more significant to Baker's project, though, was the fact that in 1962 Yates had directed seven television episodes of the Leslie Charteris detective classic, *The Saint*, starring Roger Moore as Simon Templar. In the process, Yates had set an important precedent in the numerous chase scenes involving Moore and Templar's famous white Volvo P1800—he had let the star do his own driving. Yates now cringes at the thought of shooting those scenes without the permission of local authorities and without any proper safety precautions. But when *Robbery* came along, it was more of the same, with unscripted chase sequences shot without permission in the Ladbroke Grove area of London on a wing and a prayer, albeit in relatively underpowered cars. Still in the days before stunt coordinators, Yates took his share of chances on the streets of London. A near miss with an elderly lady passing by was caught on camera and included in the final sequence.

As time went by, Yates would become known for the diversity of the material he directed during his forty-five-year career, something emphasized by that early eclectic mix of subject matter which gave him such a broad grounding. The swashbuckling exploits of Gregory Peck, David Niven, and Anthony Quinn, scaling cliffs and blowing up the bunkers in *Navarone*, were in stark contrast to the powerful storyline of *A Taste of Honey*, in which a young girl, Jo (Rita Tushingham), becomes homeless, moves in with a homosexual friend, and falls pregnant by a black sailor. It was strong stuff in 1961, yet it won multiple awards, as did *The Guns of Navarone*. After *The Saint*, Yates characteristically switched creative track completely to direct the Cliff Richards musical *Summer Holiday* in 1963. Then in 1964 through 1966, he returned to television and directed Patrick McGoohan (coincidentally, the foreman in *Hell Drivers*) in *Secret Agent,* a revamped version of *Danger Man*, unintentionally honing his skills as an action director, before being chosen to direct *Robbery*.

In the United States, *Robbery* had been well received by a leading New York critic of the day, Renata Radler. The review had caught the eye of producer Philip D'Antoni, who was working on a new project—based on the novel *Mute Witness* by Robert L. Pike and originally scripted by Alan Trustman—for Steve McQueen's Solar Productions. According to Yates, D'Antoni and McQueen settled down for an informal private viewing of *Robbery* with popcorn and beer.

Something about the reality of the ad hoc pursuit scenes—including the near miss with the old lady—must have sparked McQueen's imagination, and Yates was sent an early copy of the script. Now simply entitled *Bullitt*, the 1968 film follows San Francisco detective Frank Bullitt, charged with the apparently simple task of guarding the key witness in a Mafia trial. But when both Bullitt's partner and the witness are tracked down and shot in what should have been a secret location, Bullitt realizes he has been set up. Following the convoluted story line requires a fair degree of concentration and ultimately becomes eclipsed by McQueen's cool portrayal of Bullitt and, of course, the now legendary car chase towards the end of the movie. Yates broke new ground technically and creatively in the shooting of the chase sequence, which took just two weeks to film and is now widely acknowledged as the first of the great modern car chase movies. There's no doubt that the secret of *Bullitt*'s success lay in the determination of McQueen and Yates to deliver the "real deal" to their audiences.

McQueen and Yates were determined to deliver the "real deal" to audiences, and they left us breathless. Here, Bill Hickman takes a short flight in the Charger R/T.
Solar Productions/Warner Bros/RGA

After *Bullitt*, the cross-fertilization continued as the spotlight swung back towards the United Kingdom and a project underway at Stanley Baker's Oakhurst Productions. Not to be outdone by the Yanks, Baker and Deeley were again hard at work producing an almost surreal tale that, in contrast to the hard-bitten cut and

If you don't hanker after a Mini Cooper S or E-Type after watching this scene from the original *The Italian Job*, you need to see someone . . . *Oakhurst Productions/Paramount Pictures/RGA*

thrust of *Bullitt*, was awash with 1960s camp right down to the inclusion of Noel Coward as head villain, Mr. Bridger. *The Italian Job* (1969) became a classic of fabulous proportions and not just for the amazing car chase choreography by the now-legendary Rémy Julienne, but for the locations, Troy Kennedy-Martin's great script, and, of course, the cast. So enduring is the film in fact, that the line, "You were only supposed to blow the bloody doors off," was voted the most memorable line in any film by a 2003 U.K. movie survey. Funnily enough, Martin said in one interview that he didn't actually pen the sentence and assumes it was cobbled together as the scene was being shot.

In a business that fundamentally deals in fantasy, keeping it real may be something of a contradiction in terms, but it is one of two links between the most compelling car chase sequences like those in *Bullitt* and *The Italian Job*. The other is sheer enthusiasm for, and sometimes infatuation with, the subject matter. In 1974, H. B. Halicki, a wealthy self-made man, car enthusiast, and complete unknown in the movie world, decided that he would not only indulge his passion by making *Gone in 60 Seconds,* an all-action film about car thieves, he would star in it as well. Halicki began making his fortune at school, when at seventeen years of age he won a contract with an insurance company to make repairs to new cars for twenty-five dollars a pop. He also became an avid collector and established major collections of both full-sized and model cars before turning to film projects. Against all odds Halicki succeeded, and although the performances may not have been Oscar-caliber, the standard of the car chase action in the original *Gone in 60 Seconds* was the stuff of enthusiasts' dreams and rightly earned the film its cult status. Halicki

H. B. Halicki did what many car enthusiasts dream of with *Gone in 60 Seconds*—gathered some hot cars together and made a chase movie. *H. B. Halicki/RGA*

followed-up with a new car chase–filled movie, *The Junkman*, in 1982. The following year he brought back his original car thief character in *Deadline Auto Theft* by combining recycled chase footage from both *Gone in 60 Seconds* and *The Junkman* with additional scenes featuring Hoyt Axton as Captain Gibbs of the LAPD. Production started in 1989 on a proper sequel, *Gone in 60 Seconds 2*, but was interrupted by the tragic death of Halicki, who was killed when a water tower collapsed prematurely on set. Over thirty minutes of car-crashing footage from the unfinished sequel are included on the *Deadline Auto Theft* DVD.

Halicki does not stand alone as a moviemaking car enthusiast. It's well known that Steve McQueen's love of cars provided the foundation for *Bullitt,* and the driving force behind many major car chases has not been recognition by a studio that

William Friedkin, director of *The French Connection*, reminisces under the watchful eye of Oscar; the film received eight nominations and won five, including Best Picture and Best Director. *Author collection*

chase scenes can score high at the box office, but instead simply the involvement of a star who is a gearhead. McQueen went on to make *Le Mans* in 1971 and took Harry Kleiner, who wrote the final script of *Bullitt*, with him. Yates was invited to direct but declined, not wanting to make a car-intensive film so soon after *Bullitt* (and he has never directed a major chase since). Not surprisingly, there are no stunt coordinators listed for *Le Mans*. Instead, there's an almost endless list of the world-class racing drivers who took part.

It's no coincidence, then, that some of the most memorable car chase movies followed in quick succession, because the principals involved were the same. Director William Friedkin's *The French Connection*, released in 1971, the same year as *Le Mans*, had several *Bullitt* alumni in the credits. Phil D'Antoni produced and was joined by stunt-coordinator Carey Loftin and ace stunt driver Bill Hickman, who took flight over the hills of San Francisco so memorably in *Bullitt*'s sinister Dodge Charger R/T. Loftin, who died in 1997 at the age of 83, had a long and illustrious career as a stuntman and stunt coordinator, appearing in more than 130 films from 1939 right up until 1990.

Vanishing Point, directed by Richard C. Sarafian and starring Australian actor Barry Newman, was also released in 1971. Stunts were once more masterminded by Loftin with Hickman doing some of the driving. *Vanishing Point* was an odd film, a chase yarn that bore a closer affinity to the road movies of the era than the urban cut-and-thrust action of *Bullitt.* Newman played the part of an ex–race driver and ex-cop turned delivery driver, who was pursued by as many demons as former colleagues. The combination of the two led to a less-than-well-balanced decision concerning two large bulldozers and the Dodge Challenger he was supposed to be delivering. Loftin had his work cut out for him, although the splendid spacious wastelands of Nevada and Utah

Vanishing Point* treats us to some memorable action in this Dodge Challenger thanks to stunt driver supreme, Carey Loftin. *20th Century Fox/RGA

must have proved a less risky prospect than the busy San Francisco streets of *Bullitt.* Unlike his stunt team, Sarafian called it a day and made no more chase movies after that.

Loftin and Hickman also worked on *Diamonds Are Forever*, yet another 1971 film, along with a huge cast of stunt performers, including Bud Ekins, another *Bullitt* veteran and friend of McQueen. Ekins had previously worked with McQueen, doubling him on the famous motorcycle jump in *The Great Escape* in 1963.

Ekins had driven the Mustang for some sequences in *Bullitt* and also laid down the Triumph motorcycle in a head-on near-miss with McQueen and Hickman on the mountain road. Ekins is credited with forty-two movies between *The Great Escape* and 1998, including *The Love Bug* (1968), a popular piece of Disney nonsense in which the core *Bullitt* stunt team reunited when Ekins had again joined Loftin, Hickman, and Max Balchowsky. Balchowsky is perhaps best known among movie aficionados for preparing the Mustang and Dodge Charger for *Bullitt.* Philip D'Antoni, meanwhile, would go on to produce and direct *The Seven-Ups* in 1973, a film about an elite squad of detectives from the NYPD. In it, Hickman plays Bo, a kidnapper-cum-wheelman, but he was hired for a repeat performance of the wheelmanship he displayed in the city car-chase sequences of *Bullitt* and *The French Connection.*

John Frankenheimer directed the sequel to *The French Connection* in 1974. *French Connection II* wasn't the huge commercial success of the original, despite

The *Love Bug* may have been a fun piece of Disney nonsense . . . *Disney/RGA*

critical acclaim and three award nominations. Like its predecessor, the film contains a big chase, this time across Marseilles. In an effort to avoid the inevitable comparisons to the original film, however, this chase is on foot. Nevertheless, Frankenheimer was no stranger to high-speed car action, having masterminded, directed, and co-produced (along with Kirk Douglas and the film's stars, James Garner and Edward Lewis) *Grand Prix*, in 1966.

That film had contained some fine detail, including close-ups of drivers' feet heel-and-toeing, and it was another project that owed its success to more than a little fervor on the part of its makers. Hollywood publicist Johnny Friedkin (no relation to *The French Connection*'s director) became involved in the early stage of the deal when he was called on short notice by his friend Frankenheimer during a visit to Paris. Frankenheimer hijacked Friedkin's immediate plans in favor of a trip to Monaco with coproducer Lewis to try to sign the all-important *Grand Prix* drivers to the project.

. . . but the action was handled by the core *Bullitt* stunt team—Carey Loftin, Bill Hickman, Bud Ekins, and Max Balchowsky. *Disney/RGA*

The Seven-Ups is currently available only on VHS from 20th Century Fox. It's worth tracking down for one of the finest chase sequences ever made, courtesy of the original *Bullitt* team minus McQueen. *Author collection*

Not really a chase movie, but with some fabulous shots of classic 1960s F1 cars, *Grand Prix* **was director John Frankenheimer's introduction to shooting high-speed action.** *John Frankenheimer Productions/RGA*

According to Friedkin, they had been in a race of a different kind with another group that also wanted to make a Grand Prix movie, so they headed straight to the pit garages to mix with the teams. Friedkin recalls that by midnight they had signed their drivers and secured the project. In contrast with the list of real racing drivers taking part in the film, there were only three stuntmen, two of whom were Carey Loftin and Max Balchowsky.

The street action of *The French Connection*, arguably the most discussed scene of both films, may have ignited a slow-burning fuse on Frankenheimer's desire to shoot a truly memorable car chase of his own, a desire that was eventually realized nearly a quarter of a century later with *Ronin* in 1998. Shot in the South of France and on the streets of Paris, Frankenheimer, a self-confessed car nut, set out to make the granddaddy of all car chases with *Ronin* and said as much both on and off the record. Like Yates, his self-imposed rule was to make the action as realistic as possible.

Gene Hackman during the harrowing chase scene in *The French Connection*. For the sequel's foot chase through Marseilles, Hackman worked without a double—aggravating a preexisting knee problem and making his pained expressions quite real. *20th Century Fox/RGA*

The makers of car chase flicks do tend to move in circles and often try to top what has been done before. William Friedkin directed *To Live and Die in L.A.* (1985), featuring a wrong-way freeway chase, perhaps trying to outdo himself in *The French Connection*. Ken Bates was one of the stunt performers on *Live and Die* and went on to become a stunt coordinator on movies such as *The Rock* (1996), putting together an over-the-top San Francisco chase scene which features a Humvee and a Ferrari instead of *Bullitt*'s Charger and Mustang. But stars who appear in multiple car chase movies are few and far between (apart from McQueen and the various Bonds). A surprising example, though, is Burt Reynolds, who virtually saturated audiences with chase sequences as Gator McKlusky in *White Lightning* (1973) and its sequel, *Gator* (1976), *Smokey and the Bandit* (1977), *Hooper* (1978), *Smokey and the Bandit II* (1980), and *The Cannonball Run* (1981). Reynolds had worked in film and TV since 1959, but it was in *Deliverance* (1972) that he at last stepped onto the fast track to fame. *Deliverance* tells the tale of four businessmen whose canoeing weekend in the backwoods turns into a surreal nightmare when an encounter with local hillbillies proves that you don't need teeth or brains to qualify as a psychopath. No cars in that one; just canoes and banjos.

But in *White Lightning*, Reynolds plays a moonshine runner released from jail early to assist the Feds in nailing a corrupt sheriff suspected of murdering his kid brother. (Running moonshine, as in *Thunder Road* fifteen years earlier, provides a great set-up for car chases.) Hal Needham, stunt coordinator under John

"Ain't nobody can fly a car like Hooper!" was one of the taglines for *Hooper*, as demonstrated by a 350-foot jump over a river in a rocket-powered 1978 Trans Am. *Warner Bros/RGA*

Deliverance proved two things: You don't need teeth or brains to qualify as a psychopath, and Burt Reynolds was about to become a huge star. Many of his following films were peppered with great chases. *Elmer Productions/Warner Bros/RGA*

Frankenheimer on *French Connection II*, coordinated Reynolds' big-block Ford and did the same again in *Gator*. Needham went on to direct the first two *Smokey and the Bandit* films and *Hooper*, the story of an aging stuntman with plenty of opportunity for the gratuitous pipe-rolling of vehicles. He also sat in the director's chair for *The Cannonball Run*, penned by the automotive writer Brock Yates, who had created the real event in 1971.

Those prolific times of the 1960s, 1970s, and early 1980s did reveal one less obvious aspect of the car chase, and that was the effect the host film had on its credibility. Are the action sequences in a low-brow, fun-filled yarn like *The Cannonball Run* quite as compelling as the pursuit scenes in *Bullitt* or *The French Connection,* where the outcome for the quarry was likely to be a tad more serious? It's a bit like comparing a school sports day with a fox hunt and probably depends a lot on your fondness for Technicolor gore.

Falling somewhere in between are the Bond films, not so often acknowledged for their car chase action, but which nonetheless feature some of the best pursuit scenes of all. Except for *Never Say Never Again* (1983) and the 1967 spoof, *Casino Royale*, starring Peter Sellers and David Niven, they were all produced by Albert R. Broccoli's empire and have provided employment for countless stunt performers since the first Bond, *Dr. No*, in 1962.

Can a comedy car chase ever be as gripping as those based on murderous intent? Sure, they're fun, but anyone watching *The Cannonball Run* knows the hero will get the timing right and miss the boxcar. *Golden Harvest/RGA*

A stock car carrying the characters of Terry Bradshaw and Mel Tillis ends up taking a swim in *The Cannonball Run*. Notice the small jump ramp visible on the right side of the pool. *Golden Harvest/RGA*

The family business has made a total of twenty Bond films at the time of this writing, with the twenty-first, *Casino Royale*, in preproduction with a new Bond. The last four, starring Pierce Brosnan, were produced by daughter Barbara Broccoli and her stepbrother, Michael G. Wilson. It's no surprise that the quality of the Bond movies has remained so high, since the children took over from father Albert "Cubby" Broccoli to make *GoldenEye* (1995). Barbara Broccoli has a degree in TV and motion picture communications, and has worked her way steadily up through the ranks, toiling behind the scenes at the Bond production company, Eon, then becoming assistant director on *Octopussy* (1983) and *A View to a Kill* (1985). Later, she worked as associate producer on *The Living Daylights* (1987) and *Licence to Kill* (1989). Wilson, a man of many talents, was a partner in a New York–based law firm before joining Eon's legal and administrative team in 1972. He was an assistant to the producer on *The Spy Who Loved Me* (1977) and became a full-fledged producer on *Moonraker* (1979), *For Your Eyes Only* (1981), and *Octopussy*. Now Wilson is head of Eon Productions.

Veteran stuntman and stunt coordinator George Leech appeared in *The Italian Job* (1969) and eleven of the Bond films, sometimes as a good guy but mostly playing a villain. In *The Spy Who Loved Me*, Leech managed to portray both in the same scene, as the gunman in the Cortina chasing Bond's Lotus Esprit which he was also driving. Leech also worked on *Never Say Never Again*, the renegade Bond film made outside the Broccoli empire and the last to star Sean Connery. He was joined by his stunt-woman daughter, Wendy Leech, playing the murderous Bond girl intent on dispatching an inattentive Bond in the opening scene. *Never Say Never Again* was also the first Bond film on which British stunt expert Vic Armstrong was both stunt coordinator and action unit director, having previously performed stunts on *You Only Live Twice* (1967) and *Live and Let Die* (1973).

Up until the early 1980s, stunt coordination of Bond car chase sequences fell to various hands until one of the all-time greats of stunt driving, Rémy Julienne, took control of wheeled events for six Bond movies in a row. Julienne, who had been responsible for the driving sequences in the original *Italian Job*, coordinated the car stunts in *For Your Eyes Only*, *Octopussy*, *A View to a Kill*, *The Living Daylights*, *Licence to Kill*, and *GoldenEye*.

Armstrong was first appointed action unit director on *Tomorrow Never Dies* (1997), where he oversaw the motorcycle chase across the rooftops of Saigon; next he masterminded the fantastic stealth-boat chase scene in *The World Is Not Enough* (1999). For *Die Another Day* (2002), he choreographed the Aston Martin Vanquish versus Jaguar XKR shootout on the frozen lakes of Iceland, which involved spending about $2.5 million on converting the rear-wheel-drive Jaguars and Astons to four-wheel drive.

Die Another Day contained more CGI than Armstrong, the purist former stuntman, felt comfortable with. But for the

Wendy Armstrong—just at home pulling a knife on an unsuspecting secret agent or hopping on the back of a fast bike, she followed in the footsteps of her father, George Leech. She's a stuntwoman, of course. *Wendy Armstrong*

latest generation of car chase movies such as *The Fast and the Furious* (2001), *2 Fast 2 Furious* (2003), *The Matrix Reloaded* (2003), and, to a lesser extent, the remake of *The Italian Job* (2003), CGI goes with the territory. That doesn't mean the art of keeping it real has died. The lion's share of car chase stunt work in *Matrix Reloaded* was the real thing for which regiments of stunt drivers were hired. One of them was Johnny Martin, who, though working as a stunt driver on this occasion, is better known as a stunt coordinator. Martin was motivated to enter the business at the tender age of eight after watching Burt Reynolds' portrayal of Gator McKlusky.

Soon after, Martin would have a chance meeting with original *Gone in 60 Seconds* maker H. B. Halicki, who arrived at a car wash with the film's star, Eleanor the Mustang, in tow. Martin confided his dreams to Halicki, who patted the kid on the back and gave him an encouraging "see you in Hollywood." Sadly, it was only a few years later that Halicki lost his life, but Martin still talked his parents into sending him to stunt school at the age of seventeen as a precursor to college. Their intention was to let the boy get things out of his system, but Johnny indeed made it to Hollywood where, by now an established professional, he (appropriately enough) found himself working on *Gone in 60 Seconds* (2000), starring Nicolas Cage, produced by Jerry Bruckheimer, and coproduced by Halicki's widow, Denice.

Thirty-five years later, the next generation of MINIs is going down stairways again. *BMW GB Ltd*

Left: **Bill Hickman (left)** drives and acts in *The French Connection*. Also pictured is New York cop Eddie Egan, whose real-life experiences were the basis of the story; he had a cameo as the supervisor of Popeye Doyle (Gene Hackman). *Author collection*

Bond searches for a way out as the Ice Palace begins to melt in *Die Another Day*.
Plastic sheeting protects equipment from splashing. *Aston Martin*

CHAPTER 2
DANCING IN THE STREET

Choreographing a great car chase is a lot tougher than a few minutes of cinema action ever reveals. A look at how some of the most gripping two- and four-wheeled a moments in motion picture history were created reveals why.

"The stunt guys have a chance of losing their lives. It's a dance routine and you've got to follow every step or else someone's gonna step on your toes and kill you."

—*Johnny Martin, Stunt Coordinator, 2003*

When action unit director Vic Armstrong was faced with devising the ice chase scene in *Die Another Day*, he admits to being perplexed. After all, where do you start with a blank sheet of paper? More to the point, just where do you start with a blank sheet of ice? Choreographing a real white-knuckle pursuit scene is much tougher than it looks. Original scripts contain a simple instruction reading something like, "car chase here," to guide the filmmaker. Action footage usually, though not always, falls under the control of the action unit director (otherwise known as second unit director) and his stunt coordinators. Along with a team of stuntmen and stuntwomen, vehicle and special effects experts, directors of photography, and a legion of backup crew, they create the kind of explosive footage that becomes the focal point of so many movies. Despite the planning, a great deal of what we see on screen is worked out on the spot, depending on the movie, the locations, and the ideas people have along the way. In the case of *Die Another Day*, Armstrong knew there would be an ice chase, with a Jaguar and Aston Martin Vanquish, but the details would be left up to him, just as had been done with the stealth-boat chase on the River Thames in *The World Is Not Enough*.

It sounds easy. Fabulous frozen wastes, two fantastic cars—but, well, that was the problem. There was precious little else to go with them. Armstrong knows that lack of variety in a sequence can be the kiss of death, and this time he had no traf-

Breakthrough! The Ice Palace scenes were actually shot on the huge 007 stage at Pinewood Studios in England, explaining the crewmembers standing about in their shirtsleeves. *Aston Martin*

from each other. Even worse was the possibility of the ice being covered by a layer of snow making the exotic frozen lake in the wild and windy wastes of Iceland look no more exotic than a snow-covered football pitch somewhere in the middle of England. Armstrong made several visits to scout the location, a thousand-foot-deep ice lagoon at Jökulsárlón, and every one was made in the pouring rain. It was as if the location had its own microclimate so, convinced the whole thing would quite literally be a washout, Armstrong began working on ways to shoot as much as possible back in the United Kingdom. In the meantime, he also had to find ways of making this scene memorable. He had the cars, of course, equipped with machine guns and rockets in true Bond style. And he had the spectacular visuals of the explosions. But a successful chase would need more—a lot more.

Nevertheless, Armstrong was inspired by the few thousand acres of ice surrounded by towering blue icebergs, and pictured a ballet-like performance between the two cars—his principal dancers. Armstrong has worked with director of photography Jonathan Taylor for years, and both believed that they had found a great location the audience needed to see. Both thought it was too easy to go to a setting, wonder at its beauty, shoot the scene, finish the movie, then view it six months later and realize it may just as well have been shot in the local park.

Film people often go to locations, insists Armstrong, then forget why they went there. In action sequences, the temptation to work exclusively with graphic close-up shots and fast editing is almost overwhelming. But to make sure the audience gets drawn into the location itself and soaks up the experience of actually being there, it is essential to work with wide-angle, panoramic shots as well. And that's exactly what happened in *Die Another Day*.

Armstrong aimed to make the location one of the characters, shooting as much as he could of it from helicopters to emphasize the fluid motion of the cars sliding gracefully across the ice. The gigantic scale of the place translates perfectly to the big screen, and the glowering

Action unit director *par excellence* Vic Armstrong used to perform stunts in the Bond movies before taking on stunt coordinating duties. He was also Harrison Ford's stunt double for over ten years, starting with *Raiders of the Lost Ark*, as evidenced by the bullwhip and fedora. *Autocar*

The prototype Jaguar XKR against the chilly backdrop of the *Die Another Day* chase. Note the much-sought-after Gatling gun option. *Bickers Action*

presence of the vast translucent-blue icebergs provides a sinister backdrop to the action of the cars flashing past.

The twenty-first century hardware is in complete contrast to the icy scenery, but that's no accident—Armstrong likes to see chases taken out of context wherever possible to create more of an impact. For the motorcycle chase in *Tomorrow Never Dies* it would have made sense to use a motocross bike, especially since some of the two-wheeled action was shot on a balcony. But instead, Armstrong and his team used a BMW R1200C, its weight contributing to the story as the balcony collapses. Incidentally, Armstrong had a special reason for making sure this stunt went according to plan. Riding behind stunt rider Jean-Pierre Goy, from the famous Rémy Julienne L'Equipe, was Michelle Yeoh's stunt double— Armstrong's wife, Wendy Leech. (Armstrong and Leech had met in 1978 on the

Michelle Yeoh's stunt double, Wendy Armstrong, clings to stunt biker Jean-Pierre Goy in *Tomorrow Never Dies.* Ironically, Yeoh came to the attention of the Bond producers in the Jackie Chan film *Supercop*, where she performed her own stunts, including jumping a motorcycle onto a moving train. *BMW GB Ltd*

set of *Superman: The Movie*; he was the stunt double for Christopher Reeve while she doubled Margot Kidder's Lois Lane.)

Back on the ice, it would be easy to imagine that filming cars sliding around on a frozen lagoon is easy money, but nothing could be further from the truth. It's a huge gamble, especially for the special effects team and action unit, because with such demanding topography and innovative hardware, no one can be sure everything will go according to plan until the job starts.

Even the condition of the ice itself was a cause for concern. A few weeks before filming started, the ice wasn't thick enough, and even though its depth had grown to z the crust and sink into the black, icy waters beneath. Armstrong was taking no chances. Flotation bags were squeezed into every available space in the cars, 4x4s were equipped with ladders for reaching someone unlucky enough to fall through the ice, and even hovercrafts were on hand to mount a rescue should anything go wrong.

Ironically, what injuries there were came from more predictable causes. According to Armstrong, because of the concern over the ice giving way, Ray De Haan, the principal Bond stunt double for the chase, opted not to wear the five-point racing harness fitted to his car so he could scramble out quickly if necessary. But in the end the ice held firm—in a way, too firm. A high-speed argument with an iceberg left De Haan bruised, concussed, and unable to work for four days.

Thankfully, accidents like that are infrequent, and in fact Armstrong himself won an Oscar in 2001 for his contribution to safety in the stunt industry and a BAFTA (the British equivalent of the Oscar, from the British Academy of Film and Television Arts) the following year for technical achievements. But filming desperate on-the-edge action sequences will always carry an element of

Peter Yates, director of *Bullitt*, in his London home in 2003. *Autocar*

unpredictability, not just in the physical sense but in other ways too.

For English director Peter Yates, making *Bullitt* was fraught with difficulty, and the legendary car chase almost didn't happen at all because of financial constraints and the difficulty of securing permission from the San Francisco city authorities. Not surprisingly, the practicalities were a hefty burden also. Yates was well used to thinking on his feet in those early days when the role of stunt coordinator had barely been created. Much has been written about the making of the classic thriller with its almost unfathomable plot, but one thing Yates insisted upon was that there was no script for the chase sequence and that the whole thing was created on the spot.

Permission was eventually granted by the city authorities at the eleventh hour and then only because it transpired that producer Philip D'Antoni's family came from the same part of Italy as that of San Francisco's mayor, Joseph Alioto. It took time to find those memorable locations, and time was something Yates didn't have. Nevertheless, he would spend hour after patient hour with Steve McQueen and a couple of the stuntmen, prowling the streets of San Francisco looking for likely sections of road; the final choices were based on what they collectively felt the cars were capable of doing. The San Francisco Police were hugely cooperative but naturally concerned about what the filmmakers wanted to do.

Each day, Yates would storyboard the next section of the chase; that night he would sit down with the police and explain what he wanted so the appropriate streets could be blocked off. Storyboards are simply illustrated sheets of paper mapping the action of a scene, much like a strip cartoon. They are not his favorite method of planning a sequence for that reason, and Yates thinks their use can result in a comic-book feel to a sequence, but they are a useful way of informing other departments as to what's needed for a particular shoot.

By now, the filmmakers were almost ready to start shooting the action. For probably the first time ever, some of the stunt driving would be done by the star himself. How much of the driving McQueen actually did varies depending on which account you've read, but Yates is adamant the star did most of it except for a couple of sequences. In the highway scene where the Dodge and the Mustang almost hit a biker who lays his Triumph down in the middle of the road, McQueen's double Bud Ekins drove the Mustang in some shots and, through the miracle of editing, also performed the motorcycle stunt.

To create the fiery end of the chase for the Dodge and its occupants—the hitman Mike (Paul Genge) and driver Phil (Bill Hickman)—Carey Loftin attached the Charger to a Mustang with a special rig. At the crucial moment, Loftin hit the release mechanism, catapulting the Charger on its final journey. The idea of McQueen actually doing some of the driving was contentious at the time, and some of the stunt performers were not at all happy at the thought of the star moving in on their territory. Loftin saved the day, however, smoothing the way with the other stuntmen and defusing what almost became a tricky confrontation.

Exactly why *Bullitt* has become such a legendary sequence is hard to pin down, but there is one key reason why it made such a compelling piece of film. *Bullitt* is in a sense an early example of virtual reality where the viewer can sit right inside the cars while the action is being driven in real time. That was made possible by

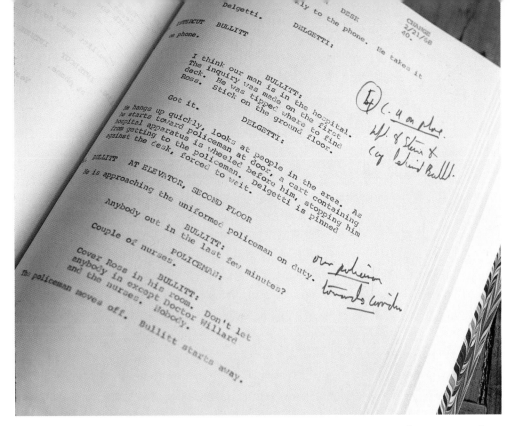

Yates still has the actual script from *Bullitt*, complete with handwritten notes, in a neatly bound volume. *Autocar*

Yates' insistence on using relatively lightweight Arriflex cameras rather than the larger Mitchells favored by Warner Brothers, which had originally been bought for making the Hitchcock movies.

Arriflex cameras were not new, but they had never been used in Hollywood before, despite being lightweight, of superb quality, and compact enough to fit inside a car. Yates pays tribute to Bernie Schwartz, the grip who did an incredible job constructing special mounts for the cameras, enabling them to be fixed almost anywhere the director wanted. Even so, the team was concerned that the road surfaces would be too rough and that the footage would be unusable.

In one scene the two cars drop down through a left-hand curve, the Charger bouncing off a short retaining wall and narrowly missing an oncoming car. Yates was keen to shoot as much as he could over McQueen's shoulder if only to demonstrate that he was actually doing the driving. Because of the violent cornering and roughness of the road surface, Yates decided to climb in the back seat among all the pipework for the camera mount so he could have his eye to the camera while the stunt was being driven. As it turned out, the ride was so rough that Yates couldn't see anything at all through the viewfinder, and he finished the day depressed and worried, certain that the footage would be about as much use as the Mustang's shredded tires. But when the rushes came through the next day, the mad dash down the twisting tarmac leapt from the screen with vivid realism. The image captured on celluloid was perfect—the camera hadn't been as badly shaken as the director's eyeballs.

That said, there is a fair degree of camera movement in most of the shots by modern standards, something that gives the footage a gritty edge that a lot of technically obsessed modern films lack. Sit in a hard-sprung ultra-high-performance car like Frank Bullitt's Mustang for real and the vibration can be enough to loosen the retinas. That's the effect Yates inadvertently achieved in the *Bullitt* chase, and, combined with the feral howling of the two classic V-8s at full throttle, it sends tingles of anticipation up and down your spine every time you see it.

For McQueen and Yates, conveying that sense of realism on film was paramount. Apart from the unprecedented move of allowing the star to drive stunts, it was the first time scenes like these had ever been shot on location and with the drivers filmed in real time behind the wheel. Photographic technique played a large part in capturing the reality too, but not through the use of special effects. Yates believes that the experience he and William Fraker, his director of photography, had gained in making TV commercials was unique in the field of feature films and gave them a profound knowledge of what the latest wide-angle and long-focus lenses could do.

When director John Frankenheimer made *Ronin* in 1998, he was determined to include a chase scene by which all others would be judged. In fact, *Ronin* ended up with two, the first shot in and around La Turbie in the South of France and the second in Paris.

Sadly, Frankenheimer died in 2002, but assistant director and friend Michel "Mishka" Cheyko remembers getting the call from Frankenheimer to come and help make the film with chase scenes shot "the old-fashioned way." Frankenheimer's novel approach to shooting realistic footage was to hire former F1 driver Jean-Pierre Jarier (veteran of 137 Grand Prix between 1971 and 1983) and current FIA GT driver Michel Neugarten to drive the two principal cars in each chase.

His stars—including Robert De Niro as Sam, Natascha McElhone as Deirdre, and Jean Reno as Vincent— would not do any driving, but Frankenheimer came up with another cunning plan to ensure their facial

Ronin* assistant director Michel "Mishka" Cheyko was called upon by John Frankenheimer to help make a car chase movie "the old-fashioned way." *Michel Cheyko

expressions during the chase scenes were as realistic as possible. Some of the cars used were British spec right-hand drive with dummy steering wheels fitted on the passenger-side dashboard. The stars would be filmed sitting in the passenger seat sawing at the dummy wheels, while stunt drivers in the left-hand seat drove them at high speed. This particular facet of Frankenheimer's approach to creating compelling chase sequences took the search for reality to an altogether new level—the look of terror on De Niro's face in several of the shots was, confirms Cheyko, absolutely genuine.

Using racing drivers to drive stunts presented some challenges, since they quite literally tend to have a one-track mind. Cheyko recalls how he would carefully brief a pair of drivers about where the cameras were sited and how he wanted the cars positioned, but inevitably a race would develop. Neither driver, it seemed, had the kind of mindset that would allow him to follow someone else. Cheyko would patiently flag the two men down and ask for a gap of five car lengths to give the cameras a chance to track the action, but within a couple of laps they would be battling it out nose to tail, caught up in their passion for racing.

The skill of the two racers produced some awesome footage, not least when Jarier had to drive through the gap left between the rolling police car and the concrete wall of a Parisian tunnel. Jarier not only scrapes through the gap while the

While the chase sequence in *Bullitt* was almost an unscripted afterthought, John Frankenheimer set out to make the greatest chase ever in *Ronin*. MGM/RGA

police car is still rolling with only inches to spare—he did it in one take. Regular stunt drivers, led by stunt coordinator Jean-Claude Lagniez, played just as important a role, however. Apart from finding it difficult to resist competing with one another, race drivers are preprogrammed to stay on the road, not leave it, so in the more lurid scenes the stunt drivers stepped in.

One of the biggest challenges in the making of *Ronin* was securing the right locations. Finding stretches of four-lane highway where you can drive against a few hundred oncoming cars is not that simple—even if your surname is Frankenheimer. *Ronin*'s location managers pulled it off, though. That particular scene was shot on a freshly built section of the outer Periphique, which loops around Paris, due to be opened to the public a mere two weeks after filming was completed, after which it would have been a no-go area.

Around three hundred expert stunt drivers were assembled for the job, which Cheyko remembers as being so easy to shoot it was completed on one Saturday. In the final scene of the chase, the character Deirdre (Natascha McElhone) puts her BMW through the ultimate crash test by flying off the end of a partly demolished road suspended in midair. This stretch of road at La Defense in the Paris suburbs actually was being demolished; the contractors held up the work just long enough for the filmmakers to complete the scene. Like many other great chase scenes, says Cheyko, the scripts for these two served only as a guideline, but it was John Frankenheimer's passion for the subject that brought the action to life. Fast turnaround of ideas, scripting, and storyboarding was essential if the scenes were to be slotted into the brief pockets of time available in the punishing schedule. Once the locations had been found, the teams had to move fast, shooting the entire chase sequences over a number of weekends.

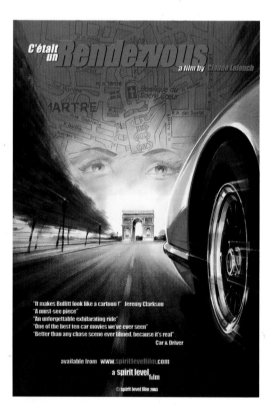

For nearly thirty years until its DVD release, *C'était un Rendezvous* was available only as a poor second- or third-generation bootleg. *Spirit Level Films*

Of course, Paris has been the scene for many great chases, such as the short but contentious battle of cars in *Le Professionnel* (1981), featuring French heart-throb Jean-Paul Belmondo doing his own driving. But there's one in particular that, even though it's a race against the clock rather than an opponent, is one of the best you will see. Consisting entirely of an audio-visual feast lasting less than nine minutes, *C'était un Rendezvous* was filmed in 1976 by Claude Lelouch, director of the classic 1966 love story *Un Homme et une Femme* (*A Man and a Woman*). *Rendezvous* may not be a car chase in the purest sense, but it demands to be included here simply because its intoxicating mixture of engine sound and dazzling action blows the mind of most people who see it. There has been a great deal of controversy surrounding *Rendezvous*, partly brought on by the filmmaker himself, who for many years chose to keep the details close to his chest. The car is rumored to be a Ferrari 275GTB driven either by Lelouch or an anonymous F1 driver (at least one industry source lists Jean Pierre Beltoise as the stunt coordinator). It is also said that Lelouch was hauled up before the magistrate shortly after the film was released.

Now for the first time, this book reveals the truth behind the story, thanks to an exclusive interview between the producer of the remastered DVD version of *Rendezvous*, Richard Symons, and the man himself, Claude Lelouch. Lelouch has

Above Left: **In *C'était un Rendezvous* Claude Lelouch approaches the entrance to the Louvre where he will swing left through an archway.** *Spirit Level Films*

Above Right: **Past the Place de Opera, Lelouch heads toward the church of Ste. Trinité.** *Spirit Level Films*

Ste. Trinité looms large as Lelouch approaches the final two miles of his course. *Spirit Level Films*

always been a man who lives for the now, someone who, when he sees an opportunity, wants to grab it with open arms. Lelouch has also had a lifelong obsession with being on time. "Every time I've had to rendezvous with people in my life I've had to be on time, it's like an illness. Even when I was born I was on time—exactly nine months," he told Symons. It is this facet of his character that prompted him to make the nine-minute film of a man dashing across Paris to meet his lover. *C'était un Rendezvous* was filmed in 1976 immediately after Lelouch had completed a feature film entitled *Si c'était à refaire* (*If I Had to Do It All Over Again*). The crew was still in town and so was the camera equipment, including the remaining thousand feet of film—enough to shoot about ten minutes of footage.

Lelouch, being Lelouch, realized this was a chance to shoot the film he'd wanted to make for a long time, and he put it to his crew that they take a car and just do it. They were tired after all the hard work on the feature and were less than impressed with the idea but came round in the end. Lelouch approached the Parisian authorities for permission and was briskly sent on his way, but the bit was between the teeth and there was no stopping the enthusiastic film director. He found a route, beginning at the tunnel exit to Avenue Foch and finishing at the Basilique de Sacré Coeur, which would take around twelve minutes, too long for the amount of film he had left. The only way he could make it was to jump all the red lights, so Lelouch called a couple of racing and stunt-driver friends to seek their advice.

One of them told him that as long as he was traveling fast enough, it was unlikely he would collide with another car arriving at an intersection at the same time—he would make it across just in front of the slower-moving car. So Lelouch decided to go for it with one proviso. Where he passed through the archway at the entrance to the Louvre, the only real blind spot, he would have an assistant stationed with a walkie-talkie to warn of any obstruction. The filming of *Si c'était à refaire* had finished in Paris earlier in the week and by Friday night, Lelouch was ready to do the drive early on Saturday morning. He called his team together, and the car (Lelouch still won't reveal what it was) was rigged with a camera on the front bumper, managed by a cameraman riding shotgun to remotely adjust the aperture settings.

Lelouch told Symons: "I didn't feel like I was the director of that film. I was driving the car and everything just happened. It was God's work." After the drive, he had discovered that there was some justification in that feeling. He was approached by his assistant with a look as black as thunder, demanding to know why he had not responded to the call on the walkie-talkie as Lelouch approached the Louvre archway.

It seems the radio had failed, and it was only by sheer luck that an accident had been avoided. The man seen leaving the car and running to his girlfriend at the end of the film is Lelouch, and the young woman is his real girlfriend. Lelouch had asked his secretary to oblige, but she was also exhausted after the feature filming and told her boss in no uncertain terms that there was no way she was getting up at that time on a Saturday morning. Lelouch was arrested by the police once the film was released, and that is partly what drove it underground, where it stayed until Richard Symons saw it and sought permission to digitally remaster it.

Symons considered a remake and soon discovered that no stunt driver would consider doing anything so dangerous. Even if they had, the cost would have been several million dollars. Nissan released an imitation in 2003, called simply *The Run*, featuring a Nissan Z racing through the closed-off streets of Prague, but it pales in comparison with *Rendezvous*—it's just too polished to have a real sense of danger, even at speeds up to 123 miles per hour. The slower, but more reckless, *Rendezvous* is what really keeps viewers on the edge of their seats.

Seconds after this clip, Lelouch was mounting the sidewalk along the Rue Jean-Baptiste Pigalle to find his way around a parked truck. *Spirit Level Films*

THE SPEED OF *C'ÉTAIT UN RENDEZVOUS*

Sumner Brown

- From the tunnel exit to Avenue Foch—514 yards (470 m), 22.1 sec., 47.6 mph

- Along Avenue Foch—1,487 yards (1,360 m), 39.9 sec., 76.2 mph

- Around the Arc de Triomphe—175 yards (160 m), 9.7 sec., 36.9 mph

- Down Avenue des Champs-Élysées—2,187 yards (2,000 m), 66.1 sec., 67.7 mph

- On Place de la Concorde—219 yards (200 m), 12.5 sec., 35.8 mph

- Down Quai des Tuileries—1,159 yards (1,060 m), 41.4 sec., 57.3 mph

- Through the Louvre to Avenue de 1'Opera—459 yards (420 m), 19 sec., 49.4 mph

- Up Avenue de 1'Opera—853 yards (780 m), 35.7 sec., 48.9 mph

- From Place de Opera to Rue de la Chaussée d'Antin—405 yards (370 m), 15.2 sec., 54.5 mph

- Up Rue de la Chaussée d'Antin—394 yards (360 m), 18 sec., 44.7 mph

- Around Ste. Trinité—219 yards (200 m), 16.1 sec., 27.8 mph

- Up Rue Jean-Baptiste Pigalle, with sidewalk detour—711 yards (650 m), 48.9 sec., 29.7 mph

- On Boulevard de Clichy—722 yards (660 m), 39.4 sec., 37.5 mph

- Up Rue Caulaincourt—787 yards (720 m), 41.9 sec., 41.9 mph

- Along twisty roads from Rue Caulaincourt to the rendezvous at Basilique de Sacré Coeur (pictured)—951 yards (870 m), 63.9 sec., 30.5 mph

Overall, the route is about 6.4 miles (10.3 kilometers) long and took 490 seconds. The average speed is 46.9 mph.

A successful chase must portray the car as the star. In *Terminator 2: Judgment Day*, Edward Furlong tries to keep one of his costars, a Freightliner truck, from stealing the scene. *20th Century Fox/RGA*

Rendezvous has been analyzed by a number of people, including Sumner Brown from the Massachusetts Institute of Technology. Brown traced the route on a 10,000-to-1 Michelin map, then estimated the distances for fifteen segments and timed the segments from the film. According to Brown, the calculated average speeds range from about 30 miles per hour on the segment with the sidewalk detour and several other slow sections to 76 miles per hour on the Avenue Foch. The average speed is 47 miles per hour (see sidebar on page 46).

Only about 50 miles per hour average? On the face of it, that sounds quite slow, but is it really, on public roads through the center of a major city? The red light jumping is genuine enough too. The sound fits perfectly with the driving action, especially through the entrance to the Louvre where the engine note echoes from the archway and when the car mounts the footpath to avoid a parked truck. What does Lelouch think of it today? He's a little ashamed, describing the film as a selfish act and totally immoral because of the danger he caused. But *C'était un Rendezvous* is nevertheless remarkable to watch, and what matters most is that the sequence was driven for real, as only the best are.

Both *Bullitt* and *Ronin* demonstrate the impact a great chase scene can have on the overall success of a film, and it's unlikely that either film would have earned the cult status they now enjoy without the sight, sound, and (if you have enough

imagination) smell of high-performance cars being taken beyond the edge of the envelope. Stunt coordinator Johnny Martin, who worked on *Terminator 2: Judgment Day* (1991), *Gone in 60 Seconds* (2000), *The Italian Job* (2003), and many others, likes car chases so much that he's devoted a large part of his career to working on them. Martin believes that a key element of choreographing a great chase is to simply cast the car as the star. In *Terminator 2* one of the stars was the formidable Freightliner truck, which was driven by a psychopathic robot. In *Bullitt*, the Mustang and Charger were a perfect reflection of their human counterparts played by McQueen and Hickman. In H. B. Halicki's original 1974 version of *Gone*, Eleanor, the 1973 Ford Mustang Mach I, definitely took center stage.

Top: **Nicolas Cage and "Rose," a Ferrari Testarossa, share a meaningful moment in the remake of** *Gone in 60 Seconds. Touchstone Pictures/RGA* Bottom: **Angelina Jolie and Nicolas Cage swap bad hair stories behind "Gina," a Lamborghini Diablo.** *Touchstone Pictures/RGA*

Many of the shots of Kowalski's Challenger racing the E-Type Jaguar in *Vanishing Point* were shot at quite low speeds. *20th Century Fox/RGA*

Despite the presence of several blue-chip names on the cast list, the same is true of Jerry Bruckheimer's 2000 remake (in which Eleanor became an earlier, though heavily worked over, 1967 Shelby Mustang GT 500, similar to *Bullitt*'s GT 390). Maintaining the pace of the action is also high on Martin's checklist. An example is the treatment of intersections, which always play a major part in all chases. Martin's rule is never to use what he calls the *"A-Team* approach" where the ND (non-descript) cars do a 180-degree spin and slew to a halt as the hero flies past; it freezes the attention on the intersection and detracts from the star car. The trick is to create a near miss, the hero perhaps clipping the rear bumper of the ND car on the way through and grabbing the audience's attention for the whole scene.

Another favorite trick of filmmakers is to "over-crank" or "under-crank" the camera, deviating from the standard twenty-four frames per second for slow or fast motion. Sometimes the results can be spectacular, and sometimes not. In *The Man with the Golden Gun* (1974), Roger Moore as Bond steals a 1974 AMC Matador Brougham from a showroom floor—complete with J. W. Pepper (Clifton James' tobacco-chewing sheriff first persecuted by Bond in *Live and Let Die*) who happened to be viewing the car at the time.

Bond finally shakes off his pursuers by aiming his car (which in fact had now become a heavily modified 1974 AMC Hornet X) at the corkscrew-like remains of a river bridge whose center section is missing. The shape of the dilapidated bridge, actually a carefully engineered structure, spins the airborne car in a perfect 360-degree roll before it lands on the other side. The sequence begins in slow motion, giving the impression of an unbelievable and rather cheesy special effect. It wasn't until a "making-of" TV program appeared a few months after the main feature that many realized the stunt had been performed for real. Another example is in the final few seconds of *Bullitt*, when the Mustang oversteers across the highway towards the camera in a lurid slide and drops its front wheels in the ditch. The speed of the car looks convincing enough, but rapid up-and-down movements over the bumps defy the laws of physics.

Under-cranking can be undetectable, however, and in *Vanishing Point* tinkering with the film speed did wonders for the performance of the already-quick Dodge Challenger. In an interview with *Muscle Car Review* in the 1980s, Loftin revealed that the cameras were under-cranked when shooting the scenes of the Challenger blasting across the desert. As Loftin pointed out, film a person walking in that way and the result would look ridiculous, but played back at normal speed a car looks as though it's really flying. In the scenes where the Challenger raced an E-Type Jaguar, the camera speed was reduced by half, and the cars were driven at only 50 miles per hour. Despite the use of tricks, however, fooling around in fast cars can be dangerous.

In the expansive wastes of Colorado, the police were happy to block off miles of road at a time, but that didn't prevent Newman from almost meeting the same fate as his character, Kowalski. His Challenger was equipped with three cameras, one mounted low at the front, another on the hood looking back through the windshield, and another on the rear bumper. With all that paraphernalia, plus a dazzling combination of the lights-encrusted camera car and the burning Colorado sun, it was sometimes difficult to see. Newman coped well until a rogue car driven by a member of the public managed to slip through the barriers, almost causing a head-on collision with the squinting Australian star who ended up taking evasive action and leaving the road.

Five Dodge Challengers were used in *Vanishing Point* and returned to Chrysler afterward in various states of destruction. In the final scene, unable to escape the police who are pursuing him, Kowalski chooses to meet his maker by ploughing head on into the giant steel blades of two Caterpillar tractors blocking the road. The car that died was actually not one of the Challengers but an old 1967 Camaro that Loftin had acquired especially for the sacrificial scene. With the engine and transmission removed, the Camaro's suspension was carefully set up so that it would track in a dead-straight line—something that required exhaustive testing.

When the time came to shoot the scene, Loftin knew he only had one chance. The Camaro was attached to the back of a 383 Challenger by a quarter of a mile length of cable and Loftin set off, reaching some 80 miles per hour by the time the Camaro reached the bulldozers. Loftin had expected the Camaro to go end over end but instead it buried itself into the Bulldozer blades before being obliterated by explosives rigged to its front end by the special effects team.

GM supplied a large fleet of cars to *The Matrix Reloaded*—most ended up like this. *General Motors*

The highway in *The Matrix Reloaded* was specially built at a cost of $30 million. *General Motors*

**Nothing is what it appears to be in the matrix—the black Cadillac Escalade in
Reloaded was really a rebodied Chevrolet Avalanche. *General Motors***

Fiddling with the frame rate isn't the only way to create the illusion of speed. Following shots, such as when stuntwoman Debbie Evans rode the motorcycle against the traffic in *The Matrix Reloaded*, can be filmed at quite low speeds. In those cases, the ND vehicles can crawl along at as little as 25 miles per hour, with the "starring" motorcycle traveling at 50 miles per hour. On screen, as the camera follows Trinity, the speed differential between the vehicles is the same as if she were shooting between parked cars at 75 miles per hour. Conversely, the same shot from the side can destroy the effect, because the buildings and street furniture in the background provide a stationary reference point for more clearly gauging the real speed of both the cars and the motorcycle.

The location was a 1.4-mile runway at a naval base in Oakland, California, dressed with timber walls, overpasses, and other props. Amazingly, most of the shots were filmed in real time, with CGI brought into play only when absolutely necessary, such as when the stunt doubles were jumping onto car roofs. Coordinator David Ellis brought together a huge team of specialist stunt performers to shoot the scene, which involved a large number of "traveling pipe ramp" shots.

Pipe ramps are literally that, ramps made of steel pipe, kept from appearing on screen by the careful use of camera angles. (Although, as with many cinema tricks, the careful observer will sometimes catch a glimpse of the device.) Traveling pipe ramps are attached to a specially prepared vehicle driving at around 25 miles per hour. A stunt driver approaches from behind and hits the ramp at around 45 miles per hour, launching and rolling the car at the same time with dramatic effect.

The level of destruction in *The Matrix Reloaded* was awesome, with General Motors reputedly supplying 300 cars for wrecking on set. GM also produced some of the vehicles especially for the film. For example, the Cadillac Escalade EXT used by the twins in the freeway scene was not in production yet, and what we saw were actually prototype Chevrolet Avalanche pickup trucks, re-bodied using fiberglass Escalade panels.

The Matrix Reloaded made the headlines not just because of the cult following the trilogy enjoys, but because this chase scene was allegedly the most expensive car chase ever filmed, costing a reputed $30 million. But Johnny Martin points out that's not actually a bad value these days, compared to the costs of filming on public roads with the attendant expense of police assistance, road closures, and so on.

Glen Boswell, a stunt coordinator in The Matrix Reloaded, had performed stunts in The Road Warrior, aka Mad Max 2 (1981), George Miller's sequel to his own Mad Max (1979). These pre-CGI films all feature an amazing amount of stunt work that leaves the viewer wondering what safety laws, if any, there are in Australia. Mad Max introduced Mel Gibson's character, Max Rockatansky, a police officer who soon leaves the force, and chases were indeed an integral part of the story. But overall, Mad Max was a revenge movie—first, a motorcycle gang's revenge on Max, for his involvement in the death of their leader, then Max's own revenge on them—with its heart in the scenes of Max and his family. Mad Max shows civilization barely hanging on, but by the opening of The Road Warrior it seems to have lost its grip.

The Road Warrior . . . part cowboys and Indians, part pirates, part asphalt dog-fight, part post-apocalypse fashion show—and all action. *Kennedy Miller Productions/RGA*

You name it, Mad Max gets chased by it in *The Road Warrior. Kennedy Miller Productions/RGA*

The backdrop of the Australian desert and its long dusty highways make for some classic scenes with Mad Max handling his Ford Falcon XB GT Coupe in search of another drop of precious gasoline. Max's Interceptor (which is based on an Australian-market Ford Falcon XB GT Coupe) is an elephantine irony in itself because the sight of eight exhaust stacks and a huge blower sticking from the hood is completely at odds with the idea of conserving fuel. (But Mad Max in a Toyota Prius wouldn't be quite the same . . .)

The Road Warrior is most definitely a chase movie, with the loner Max at the center of an extended no-holds-barred tanker truck–pickup–car–dune buggy–motorcycle–gyrocopter–anything-on-wheels chase. Making the sequences involved transposing some of the techniques from classic westerns, with post-apocalyptic bandits taking the place of Native Americans and Max's truck filling the role of a horse-drawn wagon. The chase was so good that Miller recycled it in the lesser third movie *Mad Max Beyond Thunderdome* (1985), substituting a train for the tanker. *Mad Max* had a low budget—which Miller used to good effect—but the series grew along with Gibson's career until *Beyond Thunderdome* was, arguably, too polished, losing some of the gritty danger underlying the chases of the first two films.

For Rémy Julienne in the 1960s, budgets were a good deal more frugal, which meant relying simply on skill and a lot of guts. Given his already enormous reputation, directors were always ready to listen. Julienne based his chase sequences on three main criteria: ensuring that the drivers were always of top quality, planning and executing with extreme precision, and having a thorough understanding of how reality translates into cinema. Choreography requires a good imagination as well as driving skills and technical know-how.

He remembers his six Bond films as only a Frenchman could—for the beautiful girls and the beautiful scenery, both of which made his job easier. He also had a good deal of freedom to do what he wanted, and his detailed proposals for a chase in a given scenario were then incorporated into the script.

Popularity of the Bond films aside, *The Italian Job* remains one of Rémy Julienne's finest moments, despite being released on June 2, 1969. Throughout the filming, the great man's modus operandi was apparently similar to that of his Bond work. He would visit locations with the directors, tell them what could be done, then ask what they wanted to include. In general, the filmmakers seemed to enjoy a fairly informal approach to the location work; he has been described variously as "the best stunt driver in Europe" by producer Michael Deeley (who made *Robbery* with *Bullitt* director Peter Yates) and simply "the greatest" by second unit director, Philip Wrestler.

Wrestler actually sat alongside Julienne on a trial run of the famous tunnel-looping scene—shot not in Turin but, rather unglamorously, inside the Birmingham-Coventry Tithebarn main sewer, which was still under construction at the time. Julienne made three attempts to loop a Mini in the tunnel. On the first attempt, recalls Wrestler, the car landed on its roof. The second attempt also failed, while the third attempt almost succeeded but for the Mini hitting a lip at the top of the tunnel.

The Chase Meister. Rémy Julienne (right) with son Dominique. *Rémy Julienne*

The rooftop racetrack chase was filmed on the former test track built on top of Fiat's Turin factory, which survives to this day. In one of the most famous scenes, the Minis escape the pursuing Alfa police car by leaping a gap between two of the buildings. In a documentary, Deeley and Wrestler both observed that it may have worked better had the shot been taken from a greater height. That said, the stunt work was flawless, though the intrepid Julienne recalls being given a send-off by workers at the factory who were all convinced he would die in the attempt.

In *The Making of The Italian Job*, Deeley explains how they were able to create massive jams at will using real traffic in real time. The colossal jam in the Piazza was started by blocking six of the eight entrances with "broken-down" cars, allowing the square to fill up with traffic, then blocking the other two. Apparently, the stranded locals reacted not by lynching the film crews but by passing the time of day eating picnics and in the case of one couple, making love. Other moments included an Italian location manager's somewhat relaxed approach to informing local store keepers of the intention to drive the Minis through the arcades. To his credit, he probably realized it was the only way to get the job done because many were unhappy enough about the idea to put obstacles in the way of the cars.

Rémy Julienne still works as a stunt coordinator, and sons Dominique and Michel followed in his footsteps. In 1998, Michel Julienne coordinated the driving stunts in the fabulous *Taxi*, written and produced by Luc Besson, demonstrating that great driving skills can definitely be hereditary. Father, Rémy, then went on to coordinate the sequel, *Taxi 2* (2000), with equally spectacular and highly entertaining results.

What's most remarkable about all of the great chases, though, is the apparent degree to which the filmmakers were either prepared to, or forced to, ad lib during the actual production process. Peter Yates recalls that the studio dangled the *Bullitt* chase scene "like a carrot," only allowing it to be made at the end of filming and on the understanding that production was neither over budget nor running late.

By all accounts, several of *The Italian Job* scenes required extreme resourcefulness to pull them off, and *Ronin*'s location managers were working right down to the wire to secure some of the most spectacular locations. On the carefully planned Bond films, action unit director Vic Armstrong spends a lot of time pondering his locations before scripting chases, and some of the best material is that which is conspicuously shot on location rather than computer generated. Indeed, Armstrong believes the location work

Rémy Julienne's son Michel proved that stunt work runs in the family with Luc Besson's _Taxi_ (1998). _Le Studio Canal+/RGA_

is what Bond audiences want, and he thinks that while CGI is a useful tool, too much of it can undermine credibility. He has a point. However successful CGI may be in creating virtual scenes and even entire virtual worlds, when you cut to the chase, there's no substitute for the real deal.

CHAPTER 3
MUSTANGS TO MINIS

When it comes down to it, what we all want to see in a car chase is great driving—but also great cars. Some of the most sought-after classic cars today owe at least some of their iconic status to their appearance in cult films.

"I needed close-ups of Steve, so they set up a close-up camera on the Mustang and I went along with him in the back. You can never trust an actor on his own in those circumstances because they get carried away sometimes. . . ."

—Peter Yates, Director, Bullitt, 2003

Of all the car accessories launched in the 1970s, "Dixie"-playing air horns must have been one of the most irritating. Yet they became the trademark of a global smash hit TV series that ran from 1979 to 1985. *The Dukes of Hazzard* fast became one of those curious cult icons that made you want to either stick two fingers down your throat or never miss an episode. Twenty years later *Dukes*, like many old TV shows, moved to the big screen with a new cast, but with an added twist—it was actually a *return* to the big screen. Creator Gy Waldron had based the TV series on his little-remembered 1975 film *Moonrunners*, another movie that took advantage of moonshine-running chase scenes. Waldron even used the same narrator, Waylon Jennings, in both the movie and the series. Coincidentally, one of *Moonrunners'* moonshine-running brothers was played by James Mitchum, who had previously played one of the moonshine-running brothers in *Thunder Road*. This connection was not missed by the filmmakers; the tag line on the *Moonrunners* poster exclaimed, " 'Thunder Road' was only a practice run. This is the real thing!"

The TV show's version of the story is simple enough: A family from the fictitious Deep South Hazzard County, headed by Uncle Jesse Duke and his all-American nephews, Bo and Luke Duke, conducted a running battle with the corrupt but intellectually challenged mayor Boss Hogg and his henchman, the even more incompetent Sheriff Roscoe P. Coltrane. The Dukes were on thin ice with the law already, on probation for running moonshine. Each week, millions of young men worldwide were prepared to turn a blind eye to the corny story lines for two simple reasons. The first was the boys' sister, Daisy, played by the curvaceous Catherine Bach,

The Dukes of Hazzard's Catherine Bach poses with one of the many General Lees.
Were we *really* interested in those chase scenes, guys? *Warner Bros/RGA*

The *Bullitt* Charger flies past the VW Beetle that managed to get into at least 50 percent of the shots. *Solar Productions/Warner Bros/RGA*

Opposite page: The *Bullitt* Charger's optional hubcaps—it's not surprising that they cost extra, given their magical ability to reappear on a car after flying off during a chase. *Walter P. Chrysler Museum*

whose wardrobe consisted mainly of hot pants and T-shirts two sizes too small; short denim cut-offs are still known as "Daisy Dukes." And the second was the General Lee, a 1969 Dodge Charger that was driven flat-out sideways or over jumps at every opportunity. The stunt scenes used maximum artistic license—the General frequently blasted away from heavy landings that just a few frames earlier had obviously completely destroyed the car in real life. Muscle car lovers will be horrified to learn that no fewer than 229 Chargers from 1968, 1969, and 1970 were sacrificed by the production company during the series' six seasons. Allegedly, the producers were so strapped for replacements they eventually resorted to stopping owners in the street to ask if they could buy their cars.

But it is to *Bullitt*, not *Moonrunners*, that Hazzard fans owe their thanks for the existence of a plentiful supply of General Lees. Apparently, the effect McQueen's film had on Charger sales was significant, and from the moment Bill Hickman's hands were seen buckling the seatbelt of the 440 Magnum at the opening of the San Francisco chase scene, Chrysler dealers couldn't sell Chargers fast enough.

The Mustang was suggested by car preparation expert Max Balchowsky, who also thought a Charger was more suitable than a Ford Fairlane to avoid the film becoming a Ford commercial—and also because he didn't think the Fairlane could take the punishment. As it turned out, the Dodge was an inspired choice. With headlights concealed behind a black strip of a grille, a fabulously powerful V-8 nestled beneath acres of flat hood, and that Ferrari Dino–like flying buttress styling around the rear window, the Charger had startlingly innovative looks for its day and still looks pretty cool now. Under the skin, it was ideal for the demanding job of chasing through San Francisco. The 440-cubic-inch Magnum V-8 engine was a brute that already developed a whopping 375 brake horsepower at 4,600 revolutions per minute and 480 foot-pounds of torque at 3,200 revolutions per minute. Hickman's black R/T also had the no-cost-option four-speed manual gearbox with a 2.65:1 low gear replacing the usual automatic TorqueFlite transmission and a 3.54:1 rear axle ratio and Sure-Grip differential.

The famous hubcaps that Hickman lost at least three of during the chase (two right and one left)—and which mysteriously re-appeared on the car in each following scene—were part code 587 Mag wheel covers available at extra cost on the R/T. Wheels were 14x5.5-inch JK as standard on the R/T with an 8.25x14 four-ply (4PR) tire.

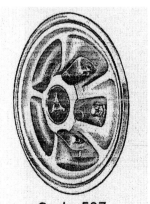

Code 587

These "Mag" wheel-type covers are optional at extra cost on Charger R/T and Charger.

A restored Charger R/T today. The *Bullitt* car produced a huge 375 brake horse-power—no wonder McQueen couldn't keep up. *David McBride*

One terrifying prospect was that even the Charger R/T came with standard 11x3-inch drum brakes on the front, which would have been totally inadequate for what Bill Hickman had in mind. Front disc brakes were an extra-cost option and fit together with 10x2.5-inch single leading-shoe rear drums. But discs did come with a booster and a dual-circuit hydraulic system.

The Charger's construction was actually quite advanced, with a unitary construction (Dodge Unibody) rather than a body on chassis. The Torsion-Aire suspension comprised front and rear subframes with wishbone suspension and 0.9-inch torsion bars on the front, and 5 1/2-leaf rear heavy-duty springs on the R/T plus anti-sway bar, live axle, and heavy-duty shock absorbers and bushes.

Dodge described the Unibody as being "better able to resist twisting and bending forces than the separate body and frame construction." But at a massive 17 feet 4 inches in length, the Charger's shell, by modern standards at least, must have been twisting like a stick of celery as Hickman threw it across the hills of San Francisco. Balchowsky clearly had similar thoughts. Although he had little idea at that point as to the brutal treatment the cars would get—except that there would be a lot of jumping involved—he decided to make some major improvements. So the Dodge's torsion bars were shortened, heavier-duty dampers were fitted, and the lower control arms were strengthened. Balchowsky also swapped the multi-leaf cart springs for some higher-rate police-spec items purloined from Chrysler.

The Mustang GT took a little more work. Balchowsky ignored the conventional wisdom of fitting a Holley carburetor to the Mustang's big-block 390/4V V-8 (4V was the carburetor type), but the cylinder heads were modified, the carburetor was reset, and an electronic ignition system was fitted. The shock towers of the Mustang were strengthened with a bracing strut. Spring rates were increased all around, and the standard shock absorbers were exchanged for heavy-duty Koni units.

All key components on both cars were magnafluxed (a crack-testing process) to avoid any catastrophic failures during the high-speed action, and both cars were fitted with Firestone tires, which on the Mustang were GR70-15s fitted to Torq Thrust wheels from American Racing Equipment. Bullitt's car also had the optional four-speed manual transmission, the Interior Decor Group deluxe interior, and a Secura steering wheel like the one fitted to the 1967 Shelby Mustang. McQueen had the wood wheel leather-covered to help him keep a tight grip.

The Mustang's big V-8 was rated by Ford at 325 brake horsepower at 4,800 revolutions per minute with an enormous 427 foot-pounds of torque at 3,200 revolutions per minute. Although the truth was that the 390's output was closer to the 315 horsepower mark, it's still no wonder these machines earned the nickname

The fabulous *Bullitt* Mustang replica belonging to Dave Kunz. *Dave Kunz*

"muscle cars"! Despite such brutish performance, the 1968 Mustang GT was offered with front disc brakes only as an option on V-8–engined cars.

Yet in the days when crash safety played a much smaller part in car design, the cars were also lighter—the Mustang weighed just under 3,000 pounds, giving it an impressive power-to-weight ratio of around 212 brake horsepower per ton, easily beating the under-200-bhp-per-ton Nissan Skyline GTRs burning rubber in *The Fast and the Furious*. Even so, the bigger, more powerful, engine of the Charger made it hard for the more famous Mustang to keep up during filming, and despite the fitting of narrower tires the stunt drivers continued to report back that the Dodge was showing the Ford a clean pair of heels during the shooting sequences.

Just two four-speed Chargers were bought from Chrysler and two four-speed Mustangs, with consecutive VIN numbers, from Ford. (In contrast, GM supplied *The Matrix Reloaded* with fourteen Cadillac CTS prototypes, two Cadillac CTS interiors, ten Cadillac EXT prototypes, two Cadillac EXT interiors, and fifty miscellaneous GM

Stunt coordinator Carey Loftin took delivery of five Challengers for *Vanishing Point*, and all were prepared by Max Balchowsky. *20th Century Fox/RGA*

vehicles for backgrounds.) *Bullitt*'s first Mustang is alleged to have been sent to the crusher because of the damage it sustained. The second, chassis number 8R02S125559, was bought by Warner Brothers employee Robert M. Ross and registered in 1968, but was then sold in 1972 to a buyer who has managed to remain anonymous and is still believed to own the car to this day, having resisted an approach by McQueen himself (and many other film and production companies since) to sell.

But despite all the hype surrounding the fabulous Mustang, it was perhaps the Dodge that lingered in the mind of stunt coordinator Carey Loftin when he started work on the movie *Vanishing Point* in 1970. He specifically asked for Dodge Challengers for their strength, Torsion-Aire suspension, and robust build quality.

Consequently, Chrysler supplied Cupid Productions with five Alpine White cars, four R/Ts with four-speed manual shifts and Hurst shifters, and one 383-cubic-inch automatic that was never used in the chase sequence. Unlike the Charger in *Bullitt*, the cars were unmodified except for heavy-duty shock absorbers in one of the jumping cars. Surprisingly, none of the cars were fitted with Hemi

Original Chrysler press photo of a 1970 Challenger R/T six pack fitted with Rostyle wheels. Go on, say you don't want one. *Walter P. Chrysler Museum*

engines, and the power and torque output of the 440 Challengers hadn't changed since the 1968 Charger, with 375 brake horsepower at 4,600 revolutions per minute and 480 foot-pounds at 3,200 revolutions per minute.

The compression ratio had been reduced slightly, though, from 10.1:1 to 9.7:1. Just like the 1968 Charger R/T, the Challenger R/T had a 3.54:1 rear axle ratio and a Sure-Grip differential. The 440 engines were also 4V, which meant they had four-choke carburetors. Kowalski's white Challenger also had the extra-cost-option "styled road wheel" (part code W21), optional three-spoke wood-grain steering wheel (code S83), and tan bucket seats. The Challengers also had power-assisted disc brakes on the front with 11x2.5-inch single leading-shoe rear drums.

Former racer Max Balchowsky was hired once again to do the preparation work during filming. This was just as well, because the cars took a heavy pounding, and Balchowsky was soon elevated to the position of transplant surgeon. Despite all the effort and the uncompromising specification of the cars, the filmmakers still cheated a little. When Kowalski accelerates away in the middle of the desert, the

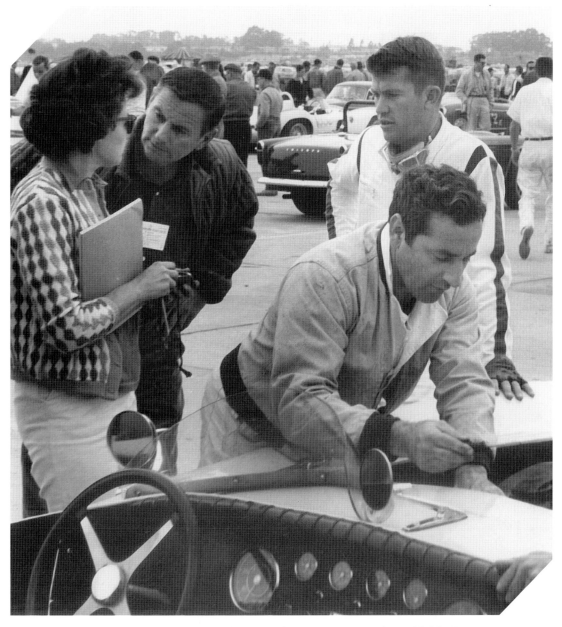

Max Balchowsky works on the No. 3 car at Santa Barbara, circa 1963. Race driver Ron Bucknum (right) looks on while Max's wife, Ina, talks racing. *Allen R. Kuhn, vintage-sportscar-photos.com*

Ray Claridge of Cinema Vehicle Services with one of the eleven Eleanor Mustangs from the new _Gone in 60 Seconds_. Ray Claridge, Cinema Vehicle Services

Challenger sounds different all of a sudden. For some reason, the Challenger's exhaust note had been overdubbed with the sound of McQueen's Mustang double de-clutching in _Bullitt_.

As time has passed, cars have moved from being mere tools of the trade to stars in their own right, and although they might not get their own dressing rooms, they might well get their own trailers. The approach to preparing the Eleanor Mustang for _Gone in 60 Seconds_ (2000) is a perfect example. In the script, Randall "Memphis" Raines (played by Nicolas Cage) and his team were supposed to steal a Shelby Mustang GT 500. But the car in the film was a special, based on a 1967 Fastback Mustang carefully modified to meet the criteria of producer Jerry Bruckheimer and art director Jeff Mann, who wanted a unique look, one that created the impression of a street racer wearing a custom body kit, departing slightly from the Mustang's conventional profile. (Early plans to use a GT40, or even a real Shelby, were dropped when they realized Shelby fans, indeed the whole Mustang community, would be up in arms over the destruction of such a legendary car.)

Mann hired Steve Stanford to do some concept drawings, and Ray Claridge's Cinema Vehicle Services of North Hollywood, California, was commissioned to build a prototype, something that Claridge remembers was completed in just three weeks. No time at all really, but then Cinema Vehicle Services is probably the biggest supplier of specialist vehicles to the film industry and maintains a huge fleet, from police cars to articulated trucks and Willys jeeps to delivery vans.

Once Claridge's men started work, Eleanor quickly began to take shape. All the front body panels, the headlight panels and the lower panels, and the grille work were changed. The hood was modified with a larger scoop; wheel-arch flares were added; side scoop upper and lower air intakes were reshaped and enlarged. A race car–like fuel filler was added, as was a stock Shelby deck lid incorporating a spoiler and Shelby rear-light cluster. A side exhaust provided the final touch and was one of Eleanor's key features, with Flowmaster mufflers and Borla tips.

In all, eleven Eleanors were built, some with fairly tame specifications for run-of-the-mill filming work and others that were about as hot as they come. By the time filming started, Cinema Vehicle Services delivered four Eleanors powered by 289-cubic-inch V-8s, and three with 390-cubic-inch motors. But with the riverbed scene in mind, Bruckheimer insisted that two cars had enough performance to outrun a helicopter, so Claridge and his team had to do some more thinking.

What they came up with was every enthusiasts' dream, a Ford Racing "crate engine" direct from the factory. The part number, M-6007-A351R, gives the game away as to its complete identity. It's a 351-cubic-inch unit with a new Sportsman block and aluminum GT40 cylinder heads with a compression ratio of 9.0:1 complete with GT40 valvetrain. Fitted with a 780-cubic-feet-per-minute Holley carburetor, its power output is 385 brake horsepower at 4,500 revolutions per minute and 377 foot-pounds at 4,500 revolutions per minute—enough to power the aerodynamically challenged Eleanor Mustang to over 135 miles per hour.

The engines are still available from the Ford Racing website and cost $5,495 at the time of this writing. The engines drove through four-speed manual gearboxes with Hurst shifters, and the cars were also fitted with Total Control pedal kits with aluminum billets. All the cars were fitted with Fuelsafe fuel cell racing tanks and Shelby roll cages for safety. The 17-inch wheels were designed in Edelbrock Cobra style for the car by PS Manufacturing, 8 inches wide on the front and 9.5 inches wide on the rear, all clad with 245/40 ZR17 Goodyear Eagles.

The interiors were all re-trimmed with stock 1967 Mustang GT trim, and the steering wheels were Lecarra Mark 3 Supremes. Four of the cars were destroyed during filming, one is in a museum in Tennessee, and another is in a museum in Las Vegas. The remaining five, comprising all three of the 351 high-performance cars, one 390 cubic inch, and one 289 cubic inch, are all still owned by Cinema Vehicle Services and are insured for $250,000 each.

Just 76 brake horsepower, but at 70 miles per hour Rémy Julienne and friends jumped these Mini Coopers over a forty-five-foot gap between Fiat factory rooftops in Turin. *Oakhurst Productions/Paramount Pictures/RGA*

Despite this apparent dominance of American muscle in car chases, back in 1968—even before *Bullitt* opened that October—a Frenchman sat in a British car in Italy intent on disproving that favorite American maxim, "there ain't no substitute for cubic inches." Indeed, as legendary stunt driver Rémy Julienne checked the shoulder straps of his racing harness for the third time while contemplating the death-defying leap he was about to make between Turin rooftops for *The Italian Job*, he may well have welcomed a little more horsepower than his pipsqueak of a car had to offer.

With a length of just ten feet, his Mk I Mini Cooper S weighed just over 1,200 pounds, less than half that of McQueen's Mustang GT. The 1,275cc A-Series engine developed 76 brake horsepower, giving the little car a power-to-weight ratio of around 125 brake horsepower per ton. But combined with the Mini's featherweight build, that was more than enough to slay a giant or two, and it was certainly enough to contemplate the worryingly dangerous stunt Julienne and his team were about to perform. It worked, of course, and the scene has long since entered movie legend—but the toll on the cars was high.

A feature written by the late Phillip Turner in *Motor* on July 26, 1969, mentions that of the fourteen Minis supplied to Oakhurst Productions—six from a reluctant BMC, two in each of red, white, and blue monotone—only four were "vaguely described as 'operable' by the completion of the picture." The Mk I had been discontinued in 1967, so when filming began in August 1968 they were already obsolete, having been replaced by the Mk II with its distinctive six-sided grille.

Despite the fact that BMC had a competitions department at Abingdon near Oxford, the home of the old MG works, the company had nothing to do with the preparation of the Minis, which instead was handled at Blenheim Motors, based at Queen's Grove in St. John's Wood, London. The preparation team stripped out interiors and installed early-type roll cages with a single rear-center bracing tube that would later cease to be eligible for competition and was superseded by twin tubes running down each C-pillar. The cars were also fitted with bucket seats, full harness seatbelts, Minilite alloy wheels, and sump guards from the same company. The only thing that didn't change was the engine, which remained the standard 1,275cc unit in all the cars.

In 1964, the Mini's early "rubber cone" suspension, where rubber doughnuts acted on steel struts to form the spring, had been superseded by the Hydrolastic suspension. As the name implies, Hydrolastic retained similar rubber spring units but incorporated a hydraulic link between the four corners of the car to compensate for the unevenness of the road surface between the front and rear axles.

In truth, competition-minded people preferred the solidity of the earlier "dry" suspension, which may have been more robust. But it was thought too expensive to strengthen the chassis for the film, and the Hydrolastic suspension took a real beating on the flight of steps outside the Turin Cathedral. Things were to get even tougher—the famous jump over the rooftops at the Fiat factory was taken at around 70 miles per hour, the forty-five-foot gap being cleared by a massive seventy-five-foot jump. No surprise really; with a seventy-foot drop below them, the drivers were taking no chances. But the leaping Minis were all but wrecked as a result, according to *Motor*'s Turner. History doesn't record whether *The Italian Job* had anything to do with Hydrolastic suspension being discontinued in 1969.

Even in standard form, the mighty Mini Cooper S was something of a formidable device. Its A-Series engine may have been based on an old concept, but the 1,275cc S version was anything but a has-been. The nitrided steel crankshaft had two-inch main bearings, the connecting rods had larger gudgeon pins, and there was a big-valve cylinder head whose valves were manufactured in Nimonic 80 steel, which ran smoothly in valve guides made from a copper/nickel material called Hidural 5. Twin HS2 SU carburetors fed the fuel, and the engine drove through a four-speed gearbox. Power-assisted 7.5-inch front disc brakes were a vast improvement on early Mini's drum brakes.

Power output of 76 brake horsepower was reached at 6,000 revolutions per minute and maximum torque was 79 foot-pounds at 3,000 revolutions per minute. That's not much, even compared to something as lowly as a modern Kia Rio. But remember, the Mini's ultralight weight still made it a potent package. Amnesiac Jason Bourne was certainly able to coax a great chase out of one in *The Bourne Identity* (2002). But the 2003 version of *The Italian Job* proved a little easier thanks to the 165-brake-horsepower supercharged engine and rock-hard suspension of the new (and now all capitals) MINI Cooper S. Modifications were mostly routine except for that of the car used in the sewer scene; thanks to an over-zealously strict application of modern health and safety laws, it had to be converted to electric power.

Stunt driving legend, Rémy Julienne shows how its done in *The Italian Job* (1969). Driving with extreme precision is essential to the success of stunts like these. *Oakhurst Productions/Paramount Pictures/RGA*

At the starting line—*The Fast and the Furious* made good use of the awesome Nissan Skyline GTR. British Nissan dealer and former Skyline racer Andy Middlehurst provided cars, parts, and advice to the filmmakers. *Mediastream/RGA*

In complete contrast to both traditional American muscle and the frenetic pace of the Minis are the cars of the American street-racing scene portrayed in *The Fast and the Furious* and the sequel *2 Fast 2 Furious*. Whatever anyone may think of the storylines and the scripting, the cars are real enough and as potent as the film implies. Most are Japanese imports and some, like the Nissan Skyline GTR, imported into the United States on the gray market where they provided a perfect basis for tuning and some truly outrageous power output.

In standard form, the Skyline's twin Garret turbocharged 2.6-liter straight-six engine puts out an on-paper 277 brake horsepower at 6,800 revolutions per minute and 293 foot-pounds at 4,400 revolutions per minute, giving a power-to-weight ratio of around 158 brake horsepower per ton for a car that weighs approximately 3,500 pounds. However, the R34's official output was said to be 320 brake horsepower, which would give it an actual power-to-weight ratio of around 182 brake horsepower per ton. Although coming up short of McQueen's monster Mustang in that department, the Nissan's handling is far superior, thanks to a trick chassis. And some road race cars are said to have been modified to produce up to 1,000 brake horsepower from the immensely strong six-cylinder engine.

The Skyline has a four-wheel-drive system that can apportion all the torque to the rear wheels and then move it to the front wheels achieving a 50/50 split, depending on the circumstances. There's also Super-HICAS four-wheel steering—the rear wheels can be electronically steered by computer when necessary, using information from accelerometers and yaw sensors. The four-wheel-drive and steering systems coalesce once the car is in action to try and save the driver from himself if he gets too carried away. Cruising in a straight line, the Skyline will be in rear-drive mode with the rear-wheel steering set to neutral. If g-sensors detect hard acceleration or the rear wheels start to spin, the system apportions more torque to the front wheels reaching a 50/50 split approaching 1-g acceleration—which is a lot. The car is designed not to understeer (when the nose runs wide), and so as the driver applies lock the computer progressively switches to rear-wheel drive. If the driver loses the tail in a classic oversteer situation, the rear wheels will steer up to 1 degree to bring the tail back in line.

Skylines appeared in *The Fast and the Furious*, but when the filmmakers decided they were to get a starring role in *2 Fast 2 Furious*, they turned to Andy Middlehurst for help. Middlehurst runs a Nissan dealership in St. Helens near Liverpool, England, and is the exclusive Skyline dealer for the whole of Europe. A former single-seater and touring car driver, Middlehurst also raced Skylines as well as testing development cars for the factory.

It was an exciting few months for Middlehurst and his crew, some of whom kept passports in their pockets ready to jump on a plane with a box of parts at a moment's notice. Glass windshields were sent to Mexico as patterns for Lucite items that were then shipped to Florida; parts were shipped overnight by courier. Middlehurst advised on a range of technical queries. The stunt crew needed to know what the weight distribution of the car was so it could be set up for one monster jump. It is actually biased 60/40 towards the front, so ballast was needed in the rear. Additionally, sprung seats were fitted by the stunt team to protect the driver's spine.

Because the Skyline's computer-controlled chassis is set up to avoid oversteer, the stunt drivers wanted to know how to make it easier to perform lurid slides. Middlehurst suggested they try disconnecting the drive to the front wheels, ensuring all the power went to the rear wheels. It worked. Early in the project, the production team wanted a brand-new Skyline. It so happened that Middlehurst had taken delivery of a bright yellow car from the factory just days earlier. The call came on a Monday and the production team wanted the car on set, in Florida, by Thursday. The Skyline was duly driven to Heathrow and dispatched by plane to Florida. In the United States, customs procedures are relaxed on cars carrying "movie prop" stickers, and the Skyline was collected from the airport and driven straight to the set. It seems nothing is too much trouble for the movie industry.

Andy Middlehurst campaigning a Skyline in his racing days. *Andy Middlehurst*

CHAPTER 4
LICENSED TO THRILL

James Bond has been thrilling audiences for more than forty years, and early cars like the deadly Aston Martin DB5 quickly became the stuff of legend. But the advanced special effects used for some of the most recent films have demanded that Bond's cars become just as special in reality as they are on screen.

"It's the insurance damage waiver for your beautiful new car. Will you need collision coverage?"

—Q, Tomorrow Never Dies, *1997*

The Bond movies may not immediately spring to mind when thinking of car chases, but of all the thousands of miles of film that must have been shot since *Dr. No* was released in 1962, a good deal contains some extremely desirable cars. Bond made a rather inauspicious start in a light-blue Sunbeam Alpine roadster. Nice car, but not quite connecting with 007's image of ruthless killer on the loose. *From Russia with Love* (1963) was even more disappointing, with a token appearance by a 4.5-liter Bentley Sports Tourer, apparently an Ian Fleming favorite.

After that, however, the cars came slick and fast, with the famous Aston Martin DB5 appearing for the first time in *Goldfinger* (1964) and again in *Thunderball* (1965). After a long absence, the DB5 rolled out from under its cover and was given a polish for *GoldenEye* and, briefly, *Tomorrow Never Dies*. In between, Bond enjoyed all kinds of potent machinery, such as the fabulous Toyota 2000GT in *Live and Let Die*, the submarine Lotus Esprit in *The Spy Who Loved Me*, and the Astons DBS and V-8 Vantage in *The Living Daylights*.

Brosnan, Pierce Brosnan, on set of *Tomorrow Never Dies* with a BMW 750iL.
BMW GB Ltd

But Bond had begun a bit of a defection to BMW in *GoldenEye*, driving a prototype BMW Z3 in addition to the returning Aston DB5—which garnered BMW immense prelaunch publicity. Though its retro-styling was startling, the Z3 was (initially at least) not that remarkable and unlikely to have been chosen by as serious a wheelman as Bond if he had been given the choice. Later, eye-watering M versions would arrive with 300 brake horsepower and devastating performance, but Bond made do with the original 2.3-liter engine that hardly qualified for serious chasing.

All that would change in *Tomorrow Never Dies*, when Bond was awarded a 750iL BMW in which to travel to work, stealing the spotlight from the Aston. Bond's 7-Series had remote control, which saved his bacon in a scene shot in London's Brent Cross shopping center. Now, anyone who has tried their hand at piloting a radio-control model car knows what a challenge it can be. The worst part is when the model is coming towards you and the transmitter controls effectively become reversed—the car's left turn goes to the controller's right and vice versa.

Imagine, then, the task facing James Bond when handed a radio-control transmitter tuned into the frequency of a real car. But if radio-control model car freaks everywhere were wringing their hands in wonderment at the skill of the Bee Em's operator, they needn't have worried. The 7-Series wasn't really controlled remotely, but was piloted by a driver tucked away in the back of the car.

The 7-Series was prepared in Munich by BMW engineers and further modified by Chris Corbould's special effects team. Engineers removed the fuel tank and replaced it with small red plastic tanks in the car's trunk. Next, they cut away part of the raised section of bodyshell supporting the rear seat and installed a steel-and-aluminum bucket seat. The steering wheel and pedals were moved back to position the driver's feet somewhere under the original driving seat. Finally, they installed a liquid-crystal screen fitted behind the steering wheel, fed by miniature video cameras in the wing mirrors and the rear-view mirror providing the driver's only view of the outside world.

Even James Bond has trouble in parking ramps—the 750iL comes under fire.
BMW GB Ltd

Q does not approve . . . BMW sedans were never intended for this job. *BMW GB Ltd*

Opposite Top: **A BMW engineer tries the "radio-controlled" 750iL's hidden driving position for size.** *BMW GB Ltd*

Opposite Bottom: **The final version of the 750iL's back-seat driving position as used in the filming.** *BMW GB Ltd*

No 7-Series BMW would be complete without a cable cutter popping from the hood. *BMW GB Ltd*

Not surprising, then, that the driver, who was lying almost prone in the back of the car, frequently got carsick during the filming of the spectacular sideways action. But there was more to the BMW than its apparent ability to function without a driver. It had rockets in the roof, a cable cutter that sprang from the radiator grille, and a rear bumper that slid out like a huge tray scattering spikes in the paths of its pursuers.

The 7-Series is now on public display as part of BMW's Mobile Tradition collection in Munich. All the effects on the film car actually work, powered by compressed nitrogen from two diving tanks in the trunk and operated by an array of buttons next to the driver. Only the rockets have been disabled, recalls John Bostin of Mobile Tradition, after they were inadvertently fired across the workshop by an unsuspecting technician. The BMW is still driven around by Mobile Tradition technicians for display purposes, which certainly brings a new meaning to the phrase back-seat driver.

Bond's final rocket-launching BMW (at least for now) came in the shape of a Z8—little more than a concept when *The World Is Not Enough* was released. The task facing special effects workshop supervisor Andy Smith and his team was a truly remarkable piece of engineering by any standards.

Chris Corbould approached Smith to see if he could work some magic with the Z8 and somehow manufacture some "new" ones to provide the film production

After taking delivery of Bond's 7-Series, technicians at BMW's Mobile Tradition accidentally fired the rockets in the showroom. *BMW GB Ltd*

All the gadgets in the 7-Series were operated by compressed nitrogen; one of two tanks is visible in the open trunk. Below the trunk are more of the 750iL's inner workings—the rear bumper slides out to reveal the mechanism for sprinkling spikes beneath the tires of pursuers. *BMW GB Ltd*

company, Eon, with the number of cars it needed. Film crews would need several cars in various states of completion because some of the scenes would be destructive and could also require filming in different parts of the world.

BMW initially supplied a bare aluminum Z8 shell from which Smith and his team were able to take molds from the front and back. Additional fiberglass shells could then be manufactured from the molds. Next they took a kit car chassis that they lengthened and widened at the front to fit the fiberglass shells. These were very much dummy cars on which the trunk lids didn't open and the front end came off in one piece. Smith acknowledges that it's hard to create something at that level without help from the manufacturer, and BMW supplied crucial components that could not be convincingly or quickly fabricated such as windshield surrounds, glass, and bumpers. Even having the correct doors to put in place saves a huge amount of work. The end result had to be perfect, right down to the door shuts and the interior. Everything had to be absolutely spot-on and indeed, at the end of the day it was.

Despite rocket-launching remote-controlled BMWs (and the amphibious Lotus), the legendary gizmos of the original Aston Martin DB5—bullet-proof screen behind the rear window, revolving license plates, homing device, oil-slick machine, Browning machine guns, tire-shredding spikes, and the unforgettable ejector seat—establish it as the all-time-great gadget car of film. That said, when *Goldfinger* was being filmed, car chasing was in its infancy. The first Bond film to really and truly meet the criteria of a car chase sequence that can almost stand alone as a separate entity within the main film is *Die Another Day*.

It's perhaps fitting, then, that the icy tussle between the Aston Martin Vanquish and the Jaguar XKR also served as the triumphant return of Aston Martin to the Bond films. Car procurement has progressed in the film industry since *Goldfinger*, and instead of struggling to prize a few relatively inexpensive cars from thrifty car companies, manufacturers are now only too happy to take advantage of the massive publicity garnered by sponsoring a film. Aston Martin was certainly eager to do

Only one BMW Z8 prototype existed when filming started on *The World Is Not Enough*. Most of the cars in the film were beautifully made reproductions. *BMW GB Ltd*

Left: **Special effects workshop supervisor Andy Smith. Just ask, and he'll make it.** *Aston Martin*

so when it handed over seven $350,000 Vanquish supercars for *Die Another Day*. The Vanquish earns its high price tag for two reasons: Aston Martin builds only three hundred units a year of its top-of-the-line model, and it's one of the most technically advanced cars on the planet, whose structure and use of materials would put an F1 car to shame.

The amount of effort that went into modifying the cars for this scene—shot on location in Iceland and England—was unsurpassed. Vic Armstrong and his action-unit team had been concerned that the rear-wheel-drive Astons and Jaguars would lack sufficient traction, even with studded tires, to perform the stunts. Hold-ups are not an option in the movie business, with the ka-ching of the cash register chiming away at a terrifying rate once the film crews arrive on location. So the radical decision was made to convert the front-engine rear-wheel-drive cars to four-wheel drive to be certain that the stunts would be of sufficient quality on the first take.

This task may sound trivial to anyone not disposed to wielding the occasional wrench, but let's be very clear on this one. Converting a fairly traditional steel-bodied Jaguar to four-wheel drive is one thing. But converting a twenty-first-century design such as the Vanquish is something else altogether.

Most road cars are based on unibody construction, the body shell forming the chassis onto which the suspension and powertrain are attached. Exotica such as a Ferrari 360 Modena are built around a welded aluminum frame, but the components for Aston Martin's Lotus-designed bonded-aluminum tub are extruded like toothpaste from giant presses by Hydro Raufoss in Norway; cut to size, assembled, and glued together in a purpose-built plant in Worcestershire using a special resin; and then cured in an oven. The idea is not just elegant and super-advanced, it's ideal for small production runs. It was first used on the Lotus Elise, then the Lotus-designed Vauxhall VX220/Opel Speedster. Now the new DB9 and the forthcoming "911-killer" V-8 Vantage are being constructed in the same way.

The front section of the Vanquish comprises a composite-and-fiberglass crash structure supporting the fabulous V-12 engine, five-speed transmission, and suspension, while the rear section is of a similar design. Svelte front and rear body panels are hand-finished aluminum, while the side panels use an advanced fiberglass system, developed in Ford's Dearborn research laboratories, called FAPP (Ford Automated Preform Process). Panels are made by robots spraying a mixture of

Opposite: **A mighty Ford V-8 engine replaced the Aston's even mightier V-12 to bring four-wheel drive to the Vanquish for *Die Another Day*. Aston Martin**

chopped glass fibers and resin into a mold that is then heat-cured and produces what Aston Martin calls an "A-Class" finish on the shiny side, ready to paint. The FAPP components are made by Brookhouse Holdings at Darwin in Lancashire, England, on the site of an old textile mill.

Brookhouse, which makes aircraft components for Airbus and the Euro Fighter, makes the Aston's carbon-fiber A-post structures, which run up either side of the windshield and resemble hockey sticks. A carbon-fiber transmission tunnel running the length of the car helps make it immensely rigid. Under the hood of the standard Vanquish lies the awesome V-12 engine developed from the 420 brake horsepower stage-one DB7 engine. For the Vanquish, Aston Martin removed forty pounds of mass from the engine's internal rotating components and retuned the engine to deliver 460 brake horsepower and a mountain of torque.

The massive engine is mated to a racing-style automatically shifted manual (ASM) transmission, so there's no gear stick; shifting is accomplished with paddles on either side of the steering wheel. With an ASM, a computer controls the sequence of shutting the throttle, opening the clutch, changing gears, closing the clutch and finally, opening the throttle again. One of the trick features engineered into the software is something Aston calls "hypershift mode," which kicks in when the driver wants to shift up a gear with the accelerator pedal mashed firmly into the floor and the engine revving above 6,000 revolutions per minute.

Then, instead of gently ramping back the throttle in the usual way, the system opens the clutch without closing the throttle at all, letting the engine race for a further 200 rpm, before cutting all the fuel and air from the engine to prevent it from going off like a grenade. Once the computer has changed gear, it brings the whole lot in again. All of it. At full power. Aston mildly refers to this as "torque reduction and torque reinstatement," but try it for yourself and you might think "ballistic" and "lift-off" are more appropriate terms.

The XKR is nowhere near as sophisticated in the chassis department and is of a similar generation to Aston's own DB7, based on a two-door steel monocoque body shell with double wishbone suspension, adaptive damping all around, and, like the Aston, Brembo brakes to do the stopping. Under the hood normally resides the sublime AJ34 90-degree V-8 engine, which evolved from the original AJ28 AJ-V-8. With variable timing of its thirty-two valves, this big-cat engine pumps out a formidable 300 brake horsepower and 310 foot-pounds

The Vanquish interior sports a massive hydraulic handbrake lever for those quick turns. *Aston Martin*

of torque in normally aspirated form, while the supercharged XKR version delivers 400 brake horsepower and 408 foot-pounds. Both are coupled to the latest ZF six-speed automatic gearbox, which can shift with silky smoothness when cruising or with a snapping urgency when the cat is on tiptoes ready to pounce.

The big Jag, then, is elderly in its conception but with a powertrain that's bang up to date. The Vanquish is a truly space-age machine equipped for the new Balchowsky age. Both have been designed at a cost of millions over a period of several years by some of the world's most gifted automotive engineers. And yet amazingly this is what Andy Smith and his team were faced with dramatically modifying in a matter of months.

Auto purists may cringe at the thought, but the special-effects wizards thought it important enough to spend £1.25 million (over $2 million) doing it. Even the bean counters at the studio, obviously no strangers to the huge cost of funding a Bond film, were nevertheless taken aback at the expense, and Armstrong admits to taking several phone calls that went something like, "About

It's not just about cars—there are also motorcycles. Pierce Brosnan as Bond and Michelle Yeoh as Wai Lin take over the BMW R1200C Cruiser from stunt doubles Jean-Pierre Goy and Wendy Armstrong in *Tomorrow Never Dies. BMW GB Ltd*

these cars . . . are we sure it's absolutely necessary?" Armstrong stood his ground, and in the end four Astons plus four Jaguars were modified for the scene. (In addition, there were three more pristine Astons and four more Jaguars for close-up work, making fifteen cars in total for a scene with two cars in it.)

Out came the Astons' V-12 and its race-style paddle-shift transmission and in went 340 brake-horsepower, 302 cubic-inch crate engines bought directly from the Ford catalog. The engines were mated to Ford C4 three-speed automatic gearboxes modified by specialist Art Carr for extra strength. Carr also modified the shift quality to make it more aggressive and added a Tiptronic-style manual shift feature. In the process, the Aston's central tub stayed more or less intact with just a section cut from the carbon fiber tunnel to accommodate the new four-wheel-drive transmission shared by both the Astons and Jaguars.

The Aston's composite crash structure was removed and replaced with a tubular steel fabrication to allow the use of a front axle and wishbone suspension from a Ford Explorer; the Explorer hubs were adapted to take the Aston disc brakes, which are visible through the wheel and therefore needed to look right. Spring struts with Spax dampers were used all around and custom-made; the torque-biasing Quaife limited slip differentials fitted to the front axles were also specially made at huge cost.

A transfer box by 4x4 guru Trevor Milner took the drive from the gearbox to the front and rear axles and was complete with a locking center differential for better traction on the ice. The Aston's amazing structure remained so rigid after the work that it was possible to bolt a rotating rig to the rear of one of the cars to film Pierce Brosnan rolling upside down. The conventional steel bodies of the Jaguars got a similar treatment using exactly the same engine and transmissions as the Astons did.

The center sections were cut out, and a complex "birdcage" framework was installed to tie the back and front of the car together. Masses of Ford Explorer parts were all shipped from a Ford dealer on the West Coast of Canada, and when the cars were all finished, they had to be re-trimmed to look like the real deal, especially the convertible Jaguars, whose interiors were much more exposed to the camera than those of the Astons.

The modified cars were tested at the Chobham test track in Surrey, England, before being shipped to location, so the special effects teams could be sure the conversions were robust enough. It was just as well, because at about the same time Andy Smith had been given his first sight of the storyboards and realized just how much of a pounding his babies would get.

All this may sound horrific, especially in the case of the very-special Astons, but car enthusiasts should take heart. The hand-built supercars from Newport Pagnell in the United Kingdom were all development prototypes whose destiny lay with the crusher rather than the showroom. At least this gave moviegoers a chance to see them in action first.

Jim Dowdall, occasional stunt double for Pierce Brosnan, stands beside the Aston Martin Vanquish. Both car and driver are ready to take care of business on the real ice.
Jim Dowdall

Last-minute changes to the Jaguar XKR's front end before going to the set of *Die Another Day*. Aston Martin

The Bickers Action crew prepares to shoot *Johnny English*'s Aston Martin Vanquish being towed away; the camera is mounted on a Super Techno Crane mounted on the truck. *Bickers Action*

CHAPTER 5
CUT TO THE CHASE

Filming car chases for real involves using lots of specialized equipment, some of which is big enough to carry entire cars or trucks. Bickers Action is a leading source for some of the most weird and wonderful equipment in the business.

"I had to jump a thirty-five-foot ravine . . . I was overheating, the bike was over-heating, so I didn't bother trying it on the flat first and just went for it!"
                                                                    —Dave Bickers, 2004

There's one thing that all the really great car chases have in common and that's reality. More recent movies such as *The Matrix Reloaded*, *The Fast and the Furious*, *2 Fast 2 Furious*, and *Bad Boys* (1995) have all relied to a greater or lesser extent on CGI. But even when twenty-first-century techniques play such a big role in a film, there are still tracking shots to be captured, pipe rolls to be executed, and core real images to be created for later computer manipulation.

As car chase sequences have evolved, so have new companies that specialize in producing the outlandish vehicles and rigs essential for capturing these sequences: high-speed cranes; endless grips for attaching cameras directly to cars; chopped down, camera-toting high-performance sports cars for high-speed tracking; and low-loader trucks that carry an entire car or motorcycle plus film crew for risk-free close-up of the stars "in action." Yes, keeping it real takes lots of special equipment and all of it is purpose-built for the job by people gifted with more than their fair share of ingenuity.

Bickers Action has helped produce over a hundred TV programs and commercials and more than forty major feature films, including several Bond films, *Mission: Impossible* (1996), *Lock, Stock and Two Smoking Barrels* (1998), *The 51st State* (2001), *Lara Croft: Tomb Raider* (2001), *I Spy* (2002), and *Johnny English* (2003). Based in Suffolk, England, Bickers Action is one of the world's best-known providers of specialized stunt equipment; surprisingly, they got started completely by accident.

The name of its founder, Dave Bickers, may strike a chord with many bikers; in the 1960s he was an internationally renowned motocross champion, riding, among others, Greeves motorcycles. But news of his extraordinary ability on two wheels soon spread beyond the mud and gore of Saturday-afternoon combat to more glamorous circles.

While racing in the United States, Bickers met keen motorcycle enthusiasts Steve McQueen and Bud Ekins (who would later become McQueen's devoted stunt double). After one performance, a sharp-eyed McQueen, spotting Bickers' obvious potential, remarked that he really should consider working in the film industry. But to the British sporting ace, the idea of a life in Hollywood seemed as remote as a trip to the moon, and Bickers thought nothing more of it.

In 1976, however, Bickers was asked by Vic Armstrong, at the time still a stuntman and budding actor, to supply motorcycles on which to round up cattle in the lowbrow family adventure movie *Copter Kids*. Bickers had the first opportunity to get involved with something more specialized than motorcycles in 1978. This time he was sent to Sweden on a mission to investigate hydrocopters, machines capable of skimming across both ice and water for the film of Alistair McLean's thriller *Bear Island*, starring Donald Sutherland and Vanessa Redgrave. The idea, though, was to use them on soft snow, something for which they were not designed.

Bickers soon discovered that the engines lacked the power to get the heavy machines planing on the surface of the snow, so his next stop was California to search out some turbochargers to soup up the puny VW motors. It worked, and the 'copters now flew across the surface of the snow at a frightening pace. Bickers learned the practical realities of filming great action sequences at that time. Filming in Canada involved living in tents at four thousand feet above sea level for five to six weeks at a stretch, living four to a tent. The hydrocopters proved too heavy for helicopters to lift up the mountain, so they had to be disassembled, transported to the mountaintop, and painstakingly reassembled. But they made it, and several near accidents with Bickers at the controls all made it to the final cut and spiced up the action.

Armstrong called Bickers again to help out on *Escape to Athena* (1979) after a motorcycle stunt rider had injured himself in a crash. Bickers doubled

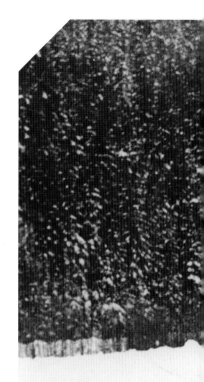

Bickers was called by Vic Armstrong for Alistair McLean's *Bear Island* (1978) to tune up the weird and wonderful hydrocopters to run on snow instead of water. *Bickers Action*

Dave Bickers doubling for Elliott Gould in *Escape to Athena* (1979). *Bickers Action*

for Elliott Gould riding a motorcycle with sidecar, dressed as a World War II German soldier.

Naturally, the drab-painted motorcycle combination was actually no tired old BMW R75, but a disguised state-of-the-art Wasp-BSA 650cc motocross outfit which Bickers had brought along with him. The first task was to jump a donkey and cart; next up was a thirty-five-foot ravine. The weather was stiflingly hot and made worse by the costume, which included a greatcoat and leather jackboots. Each time Bickers expected the director to shout, "action!" he'd have to stand down while the crew ironed out more details. By the time everything was ready, the engine was overheating and so was Bickers. Fed up with the heat and with no practice on the flat, Bickers decided to go for the jump then and there, landing safely in front of a cheering and thoroughly impressed crew.

Left to right: Vic Armstrong, Dave Bickers doubling Eva Marie Saint, and the late Mark Boyle in *The Curse of King Tut's Tomb* (1980). *Bickers Action*

Slowly the requests started to flow in, and Bickers realized just how much trouble people were having trying to rig things for chase and stunt sequences. He started Bickers Action to help them out and has never looked back. Now his son, Paul, runs the business, which has grown to accommodate 4,500 square feet of custom-built workshops. A further 57,000 square-foot test area can accommodate full-size on-set test beds and provided the venue for dry testing the barrel-rolling black speedboat in *The World Is Not Enough* before trying the stunt for real on the River Thames.

What do filmmakers do if a car chase scene calls for filming the star—whose driving isn't so hot—first through the windshield and later pulling up alongside him in another vehicle? They use a forty-foot low loader with air-cushion suspension. The car is driven onto the back of the trailer with its front wheels on spinners, enabling the actor to twirl the wheel around. The film crew is installed at the front of the trailer secure within safety rails and enough scaffold tube to rig their cameras. If they want, they can use an optional universal car rig to attach hood and door camera mounts while an onboard generator provides all the power.

Paul Bickers and father, Dave, today. *Jesse Crosse*

The low loader moves off in the hands of a skilled driver, the car bounces a little on its suspension, the scenery rushes by, and the actors sit in the car and act. For the really heavy stuff, there's an articulated truck big enough to carry small trucks on its back. Everything is accomplished with complete control and absolute safety—it's predictable, which is essential in the world of moviemaking, because unpredictability costs money.

For motorcycle scenes—as always, the star is too expensive to take risks with— a banking rig provides some real action and also allows accurate photography. An A-frame attaches to the front forks of the bike, allowing an actor to be towed behind a tracking vehicle and banked from side-to-side without the star actually having to control the bike. This rig from Bickers is a unique design and saw action in *Tomorrow Never Dies.*

The team can do much the same thing with cars, also by attaching an A-frame to the front suspension. The car is towed by a truck but, unlike when the low loader is used, rolls along the ground on its own tires. The actor may appear to be driving, but actually has no control over the car at all.

For all-around tracking, an Air Ride Chevrolet Silverado V-8 six-wheeler can be outfitted with a crane and carry seven people on its working deck. In addition to all these heavy machines, the Bickers Action team is backed up by a host of pint-sized equipment. There are small camera-carrying quad bikes for tracking shots on poor terrain, a motorcycle-and-sidecar combination for the same job, and a tiny chopped-down Citroën 2CV for very smooth tracking work. There's even an electric

Shooting a London cab in London's Portobello Road using a low loader. *Bickers Action*

If you thought they'd risk two such valuable cars to actors, think again.
The Ferrari F355 and DB5 rigged on an A-frame for the side-by-side shots
in *GoldenEye. Bickers Action*

golf caddy for silent tracking, which is ideal for filming people on bicycles—not that we see too many of those in car chases. (Although there is a rather amusing car and bicycle chase scene near the end of the animated 2003 film *The Triplets of Bellville*.)

At the high end of the Bickers spectrum are high-performance tracking vehicles such as the TVR Tasmin 350i. Its 3.9-liter 197–brake horsepower V-8 will punt it to 60 miles per hour in just 6.1 seconds and the quarter mile in 14.8 seconds—complete with camera crew. Part of the chase sequence through the multi-story parking ramp in *Tomorrow Never Dies* was filmed from the back of the Tasmin, with the film crew firmly strapped into twin bucket seats by safety harnesses.

The Tasmin, although sometimes more spectacular than the cars it is filming, couldn't carry the weight Paul Bickers wanted, and the team decided it was time to build an even safer, more spacious vehicle without compromising performance. The replacement was a 1986 750iL BMW powered by BMW's awesome 5-liter 350i 300–brake horsepower V-12 engine, which cost over $170,000 new. The combination of long wheelbase, automatic gearbox, self-leveling suspension, and payload of just over half a ton make it perfect for the job. Perfect, that is, once the car had been drastically modified, turning it from a luxury limo into one of the world's poshest pickup trucks.

Above left: **A modified Porsche 928 tracking vehicle goes into action at the Paul Ricard Grand Prix circuit in the South of France.** *Bickers Action* Above right: **It may look like a Mini Moke (a Jeep-like version of the original Mini Cooper), but it's a formidably quick TVR 350i insert car.** *Bickers Action*

The Bickers Action crew on location with a quad tracking vehicle. *Bickers Action*

In *I Spy* the team worked for special-effects expert Terry Glass on a chase sequence where Eddie Murphy had to "offload" himself from a moving car hauler. Apart from crashing into an awful lot of cars with a huge truck, the scene also required Murphy to use his car as a battering ram to shift the other cars out of the way. The cars flipping from the back of the hauler were helped along with nitrogen rams built by Bickers' engineers.

Quad bikes carried camera crews during the filming of the movie *The 51st State*, which involved a moderately complex car chase and a month's filming for the Bickers' company. The scene mainly consisted of a Vauxhall Omega police car chasing villains in a Jaguar XJ6 (what else?) through the narrow alleyways of Liverpool, England. Bickers Action also used a combination of the Tasmin and low loader for that job, which culminated with the Jaguar jumping from the dockside onto a barge in the River Mersey.

There's more to a car sequence than simply chasing and rolling, of course. Gratuitous destruction usually plays a large part of the action too, but preparing for it is more complex than it may appear. At one point in *Mission: Impossible*, a parked car is blown apart in the street. Sounds simple, but the effect involved not one but two destructive components. Working with the special effects teams, Bickers Action engineers equipped the car with a powerful nitrogen cannon to lift the car to a height of twenty-five feet while spinning it around. At the same time,

The new hugely fast and safe BMW 750i V-12 insert taking shape in the workshop. It's now up and running. *Bickers Action*

The TVR takes on a Formula One car. They did say it was fast . . . *Bickers Action*

the special effects team detonated charges built into the car, creating the impression that it had been blown into the air by an assassin's bomb.

Bickers Action has three 8.25-ton workshop trucks for jobs such as these and performed the whole task on location in Prague. Two cars were prepped just in case, which involved removing the fuel tanks and all other flammable materials before cutting a hole in the floor and installing the cannon. The cars were sourced and supplied by Action Cars of Harrow, England, which actually meant the blowing up of a car in the center of Prague for an American-made movie ended up becoming something of a British affair.

The mechanics that helped the black jet boat perform its airborne roll above the Thames in *The World Is Not Enough* were the idea of Dave Bickers. The initial jump attempts, using ramps to initiate the roll, met with little success. Then Bickers came up with the idea of using jets of compressed nitrogen to spin the boat like a giant aquatic Catherine wheel. It was tested in the Bickers yard by dangling

"Just nipping down to the shops, dear." A nitrogen cannon sends an old Ford Sierra into orbit. *Bickers Action*

Ballast on the nose makes the car pitch forward, but the force breaks its back.
Bickers Action

the boat nose-first from a crane and firing the jets to see if it would spin. It worked superbly. The Tasmin was pressed into action for the tracking work from the riverside, and the day of filming was a huge success.

While an entire fleet of outlandish vehicles designed to cover every aspect of filming forms a crucial part of the Bickers armory, there's an equally impressive array of stunt equipment and mechanical special effects to go with them. The nitrogen cannon used on the car in Prague is one example, but there are dozens more. In fact, nitrogen cannons play a key part in the stunt business, another example being the roll-over cannon used to turn over any kind of vehicle the director chooses, from a MINI to a tractor-trailer. Nitrogen straight-fire cannons have a similar role but, as the name suggests, are used to propel the car in a straight line, not just along the ground but high into the air as well. Cannons involve installation into the car, however, so there is a simpler option.

The pipe ramp is one of the favorite tools in the car chaser's workshop, and if it can be hidden from the camera's view it's an easier method of launching and rolling a car. Made of steel piping, it's portable and can be positioned out of sight behind, for example, another car. When you see a car colliding with another, launching into the air, and rolling over, you can bet a pipe ramp was responsible. Rolling pipe ramps do a similar job but allow the stunt to be performed with both cars moving.

If you want to capture the reaction of the actor in a spinning car, the easiest method is to mount the car on a motorized stunt turntable. "Wheel Skate Go Jacks" can be fitted to the rear of cars, making it easy to simulate handbrake turns in confined spaces. A portable rolling road with hydraulically powered rollers is ideal for simulating driving while the car sits in place—the rollers spin its wheels so the car's engine doesn't need to be running. To really shake things up, there's the "Spit Roast Rig," in which a cut-down car is mounted to simulate a rollover with the actors inside; a camera revolving with the car captures all the action.

If it sounds like a difficult and complicated business, it is. It's no wonder that production companies are becoming more interested in using CGI to simulate real action. Thankfully, that's something special effects experts are resisting, because while CGI is great for animation, there's nothing quite so compelling as real stuntmen and stuntwomen performing real stunts in real cars. And when it comes to filming a great car chase, just remember, it's reality that counts.

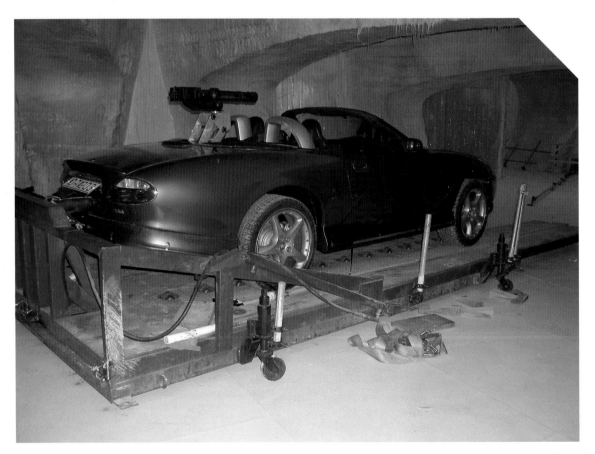

Above: **A Bickers Action Spit Roast Rig simulates a rollover without damaging expensive artists.** *Bickers Action* Opposite page: **The Jaguar XKR ready for blasting through the Ice Palace under nitrogen power. The cannon's ram is inserted beneath the rear license plate.** *Aston Martin*

CHAPTER 6
LIGHTS, CAMERA, ACTION!

One of the reasons people like to sit in a darkened theater and immerse themselves in a good film is that it allows them to escape from reality for a couple of hours. Actually capturing the images on film is the cinematographer's job. He's backed up by a team of grips whose task is to mount the camera anywhere the director wants it. And if you were thinking that all it takes is to set up the cameras, point them at something, and reach for the megaphone, then read on.

"The most important aspect of filming car chases is to make them different every time. That's the whole thing—everything has got to be fresh, and you must try to put as many original elements into each chase as you possibly can."
—Harvey Harrison, Cinematographer, 2004

These days, most of us have added a camcorder to our collection of must-have gadgets. They're great fun for capturing some of those moments that might otherwise slip into the mists of time, and if you are the adventurous type you may even have a go at something more ambitious. But no matter how much modern technology might flatter to deceive, few of us are going to become legendary moviemakers—overnight particularly—when it comes to creating really memorable images.

Cinematography is an art form ranking alongside painting, sculpture, and still photography. Trouble is, because motion pictures are such complex creations, that fact is sometimes lost on audiences who may stop registering the credits much beyond the leading artists. Nevertheless, the cinematographer's role is crucial. He or she is responsible, in more ways than one, for creating the image that appears on screen.

On a technical level, the cinematographer (also known as the director of photography or DP) is in charge of the entire camera department, including lighting and the grips—the people who mount cameras wherever the director and cinematographer require. They are also the one person on the floor of the set who can field answers to most questions and leave the director unburdened.

After forty years in the business, cinematographer Harvey Harrison is at the top of his game. The shiny thing is one of the tools of his trade, a large light reflector for filling in dark areas of a shot. *Harvey Harrison*

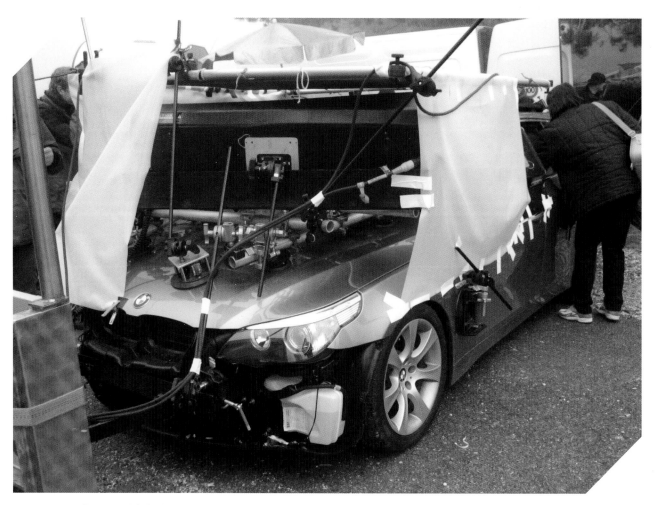

So you think those through-the-windshield shots are simple? This BMW 5-Series is rigged for shooting a TV commercial. The camera is behind the plastic sheets, which diffuse natural light. *Camera Revolution*

On a creative level, the cinematographer works closely with the director on every aspect of making the shot, including framing and, if necessary, lighting. They are supported by the production designer, whose work on set will be completed before shooting begins, and the storyboard artist, who renders the director's vision of how the shots in a scene will look in a cartoon strip–style sequence of drawings.

The differences between filming the closely interactive scenes between actors and shooting action sequences is so great that in all large feature films there are two completely separate film units. The second unit, or action unit, is controlled by the second unit director—a specialist in filming action sequences and pulling together the experts required to make them happen. The film's director will discuss with the second unit director what he wants, and the second unit director will make the decisions needed to create the footage. It's possible the main unit's director will have no experience in filming action at all and will rely completely on his second unit director to produce the goods.

Many of the most experienced cinematographers have enjoyed hugely varied careers and are valued for the immense experience they have gained in many dif-

Inside the diffusing screens, an Arriflex 435 is rigged to shoot through the BMW's windshield. *Camera Revolution*

ferent aspects of filmmaking. Commercials often form part of a cinematographer's background, just as they have with some directors. Royal College of Art graduate Sir Ridley Scott—director of *Alien* (1979), *Blade Runner* (1982), *Thelma & Louise* (1991), and *Black Hawk Down* (2001)—spent a number of years directing TV commercials before moving on to feature films. His ability to produce graphic visualizations in storyboard form yielded immediate results; the sinister sets of *Alien* and *Blade Runner* are a testament to his fantastic imagination (and the dark genius of H. R. Giger and the futurism of Syd Mead, respectively). Peter Yates and William Fraker (cinematographer on *Bullitt*) both had experience in shooting commercials, and Yates attributes some of his success with the cult film to the camera techniques he and Fraker learned during that period of their careers.

Harvey shoots an action sequence in the 2004 action film *Sahara*.
Harvey Harrison

Harvey Harrison has worked in the film industry for over forty years, starting as a camera operator in the 1960s, then becoming a cinematographer and second unit director. His experience includes TV commercials for cars, including a car chase for a Mini commercial shot in Amsterdam and following hot on the heels of *The Italian Job* (1969). He also spent ten years filming F1 Grand Prix racing for TV and feature videos, finally becoming involved mainly in feature films in 1994.

Harvey is widely sought after as one of the most experienced cinematographers in the business, working mostly in the second unit on action material. His summary of how to photograph a memorable car chase is refreshingly straightforward: First, always go for the most dramatic angle you possibly can in every shot. Second, the car being filmed is obviously chasing or being chased, but following just that car for too long can be dull (as sometimes happens in F1 coverage where the focus often remains on the leader). Capturing the interaction between the chase car and the lead car is the key, whether panning from one to the other, tracking both in the same shot, or keeping one in the background and pulling focus—shifting the sharp focus of the image from foreground to background within the same shot.

Lighting is often the least complicated aspect of making a car chase since most are filmed in daylight. There are exceptions, though, such as the need to light an actor's face in close-up; in that case the shot may be completed on a low loader to give the film crew complete control. It's useful if the actor can drive and act at the same time, because the camera can be attached to the car for a live shot, but those opportunities are few and far between.

In general terms, it is unnecessary to record sound while shooting a car chase, except sometimes "wild sound," which is not synchronized with the film. Accordingly, the cinematographer will use a wild camera, so called because it does not record synchronous sound at all. Wild cameras are far more versatile than sync-sound cameras. They can be run at many different speeds (anything from 1 to 150 frames per second), can easily perform automatic speed changes, and allow easy adjustment of focus and shutter settings. Most important of all, because they don't incorporate bulky sound insulation to avoid the camera's mechanism being recorded on the soundtrack, they are small, adaptable, and fit into tight spaces.

The most popular wild camera is the German Arriflex 435, which Harvey describes as a high-quality adaptable camera. It's so good, in fact, that filmmakers rarely use anything else in any shot that doesn't require synchronous sound. The Arriflex 535 or the Panaflex in the United States are both examples of sync-sound cameras that are better suited for studio work.

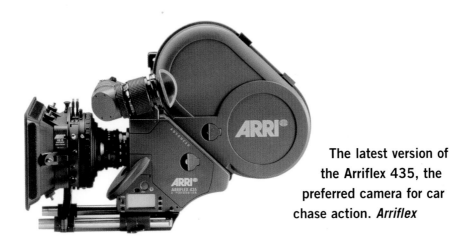

The latest version of the Arriflex 435, the preferred camera for car chase action. *Arriflex*

Toyota Hilux rigged for the ice chase in *Die Another Day*. The doors have been removed for easy exit in case the ice collapses. *Bickers Action*

The 535 can hold a massive thousand feet of film lasting eleven minutes running at roughly ninety feet a minute. In contrast, a 435 may be used with a less cumbersome four-hundred-foot magazine. All three cameras take 35mm film, the most popular format for feature films, though 16mm is still occasionally used on some low-budget films. In the past, directors would have to wait for the daily rushes—the raw and unedited footage—to be processed in order to verify that the shot had been successful. Today, most 35mm cameras have video feeds from the eyepiece to a lightweight Sony "clamshell" recording deck, enabling the director to watch video playback instantly.

Once the choice of camera has been made, the cinematographer has to decide on the lens. Many different types of lenses are still used in a single film and are produced by a number of manufacturers: Arriflex lenses are made by the legendary German firm Carl Zeiss AG; Panavision makes their own lenses; British manufacturer Cook makes lenses known for their slightly softer, warmer look; while the French company Angenieux only makes zoom lenses.

Some lenses create harder images, some softer, depending on the optics. Some have subtler steps between angles than others and some deal with harsh light conditions better than others. Making the right choice to deliver the feel that both the cinematographer and the director want requires years of experience. Whatever the final choice, both the main and second unit director will use the same lenses to ensure continuity throughout the film.

Cinematographers draw on a basic kit known as "prime lenses" comprising as many as seven different lenses with focal lengths between 18mm and 100mm. Lenses can be as wide as 10mm or 14mm, while telephoto lenses can have a focal length of 1,000mm. Zoom lenses also come in a range of sizes. One may operate between 18mm and 100mm, while another may zoom from 24mm to 240mm or 150mm to 600mm and so on. The cinematographer also has to consider the aperture of a lens and how that affects its light requirements. Longer (telephoto and zoom) lenses tend to have a smaller aperture and therefore need more light.

While the cinematographer chooses lenses, he or she also has to consider film speed. The speed is measured in ASA (American National Standards Institute) and relates to the film emulsion's sensitivity to light; the higher the number, the "faster" or more sensitive the film. So the less light there is, the faster the film you need to use. In the past, using a faster film speed meant a trade-off in quality, the

Above left: **The Arriflex 535B sound-synch camera. *Arriflex***
Above right: **A Libra mount with an Arriflex 435 attached to a crane to shoot tracking shots for an Aston Martin corporate production. *Camera Revolution***

A Bickers Action Silverado equipped with crane, Libra mount, and Arriflex 435 for a car commercial shoot. *Bickers Action*

image quality becoming more grainy as the speed increased. Today, Kodak film is available in a wide range of speeds from 50 ASA to 800 ASA, but current high-speed film is far less grainy than it used to be. Should a cinematographer want to exaggerate the hardness of bright light conditions, then a slow 50 ASA stock will emphasize that characteristic. If he wants to soften the contrast of the light, a faster film stock should do the trick, in addition to the appropriate choice of lenses.

Filters are another essential ingredient. A neutral filter set in front of the lens can knock back the intensity of a too-bright sky. A blue filter will enrich a blue sky, whereas an orange hue might improve the color of a sunset. Polarizing filters have the same effect as a pair of Polaroid sunglasses, killing glare and producing rich, saturated colors. At the time of this writing, Harvey had just finished working on *Sahara* (2004) as second unit DP. The main unit cinematographer wanted to give the entire picture a golden hue to highlight the location, so the filter company made a special filter blend for them called "Sahara Gold."

Sahara has just about every chase in it imaginable, from helicopters to boats and cars to tanks. The complexities of shooting fast-moving action sequences can be technically demanding. Things do go wrong, but Harvey's approach is simply to take it on the chin. If the car you are about to shoot breaks, then bring on the backup. If that's not possible, go and work on another shot altogether. The main thing is to keep the momentum going and the crew busy. Apart from anything else, keeping the work moving is better for morale on the set.

The hydraulic rig fitted to the front of this Land Rover carries a Libra 3 mount fitted with an Arriflex 435 camera during the filming of *Sahara*. The rig allows the camera to float up and down relative to the Rover as it travels over the undulating terrain, yielding a more stable shot. *Bickers Action*

An ATV equipped with a Libra 3 mount carrying a 65mm camera, noticeably larger than the usual 35mm movie camera. *Bickers Action*

As far as chase techniques go, it is important to come up with varying camera angles, different shots, and new ideas. Everybody joins the think tank—including the second unit director, the director of photography, and the camera operator—in order to produce something fresh. It keeps getting harder, and Harvey admits we're reaching the stage where most things have been tried at some stage or another. The situation and the location help a lot and sometimes even determine what will happen. In *Sahara*, a conventional car—not a 4x4—was being chased across the desert by a helicopter. It got bogged down and stuck in the sand much as you would expect. There were a lot of physical problems to overcome, but ultimately the situation added to the end result.

Cinematographers have a substantial team of expert specialists to handle every detail of the mechanical side of filming. One of the most crucial tasks falls upon the grips, whose job it is to mount cameras anywhere the director and DP require. That may sound straightforward—and sometimes it is—but more often than not grips and their riggers will be called upon to mount cameras in some extreme locations. It doesn't stop with cars; cameras may need to be, for example, attached inside the roof of a large building perhaps eighty or ninety feet high.

Chief grip John Fleming on location in Thailand. *John Fleming*

Time is of the essence, so grips need to work fast and be adaptable. Cars often need to be rigged in one or two hours, and exactly what's required depends a lot on the type of driving the rig will be subjected to. Gentler work on smooth roads may be followed by an off-road shot or with stunt drivers moving at high speed and cornering hard, so grips have to be ready for anything.

John Fleming is a chief or key grip who owns all his own equipment, which he usually transports in two 17.5-ton trucks. The gear can comprise almost anything—platforms, dollies, car rigs, cranes, specialized rigs to attach cameras in awkward places, tracks—you name it and Fleming will probably have it. Included in his gear is a custom car rig he's developed over the years. In the very early days, car rigs were made of timber or scaffolding tube. Fleming's custom-designed car rig is mostly fabricated from scratch using special 52mm tubing. These days, specialized shops supply universal car rigs, but Fleming's can be attached to cars, fairground rides, tanks, boats, or planes and can accommodate any camera. The rig is attached by suction cups or the masses of specialized clamps and fixings Fleming has accumulated and manufactured himself.

John Fleming's purpose-built rig attached to a BMW. *John Fleming*

Above: **A Doggicam Sparrow Head 400 with an Arri IIC prepare to go cruisin' for a bruisin' onboard a NASCAR Chevy.** *Doggicam Systems*
Below: **The latest lightweight camera from Arriflex, the 235, is likely to become the preferred camera for filming car chase action.** *Arriflex*

Andy Friswell, a highly experienced grip who has worked on a huge variety of action and chase films, explains that the usual approach is to weld or bolt the pipe fittings to the underside of the car. Next, pipework is clamped to the fittings, forming an extremely rigid cage right around the car, sometimes braced onto the roof rack fittings. Some of the cars Friswell has worked on presented their own special problems—especially supercars such as Lotuses or Ferraris. On one occasion, the ground clearance of a Lotus Esprit V-8 prevented the traditional approach, so Lotus was called in to make some special body panels complete with mounting points for the rig. Generally, cars arrive from specialist suppliers accompanied by car prep people who do most of the mechanical work.

The carbon-fiber Doggicam Sparrow Head 200 mount holds an Arri IIC camera, the complete unit weighing just thirty-two pounds. *Doggicam Systems*

Once a car is rigged, it's time to fit the cameras. For action footage the choice is likely to be the Arri 435, although the latest lightweight camera from Arriflex, the smaller 235, may well become a favorite in the future. In risky situations where the camera may become damaged, filmmakers may choose an older camera such as the Arri III or IIC, as long as it's possible to live without some of the sophisticated features available on the 435. The U.S. firm Doggicam produces a modified ultra-lightweight version of the Arri IIC, which is ideal for high- or low-tracking use right down to two inches from the ground! Doggicam also makes lightweight Sparrow Head mounts for attachment to motorcycles, cars, or other moving machinery.

How the camera is physically attached to its rig depends a lot on the type of footage the cinematographer and director are after. Usually, it will be mounted using a stabilized head, some of which are equipped with gyros, while others, such as Camera Revolutions' Libra Mk IV, are stabilized electronically. Stabilized heads do exactly what the name suggests. They keep the camera level on all axes whatever the tracking vehicle is doing. Fleming recently used a self-assembly tower crane to allow a gyro-stabilized camera to smoothly move two hundred feet during a shot while suspended fifty feet above the ground. For a slightly more robust result, the camera plate may be clamped in place using small rubber washers to allow a tiny amount of movement.

Cinematography is a complex art form and on a full-blown feature film involves a vast team of production people to make it all happen. Committing a car chase sequence to celluloid, however short, requires not just huge original creative input from the director, the director of photography, and his team, but also enormous technical input from experienced grips and riggers. So the next time the latest must-see sequence hits the theaters, spare a thought for the skills of these backroom boys and girls. Without them, none of those classic car chase scenes would ever have come about.

Opposite Top: **A Doggicam Sparrow Head 400 mount with an Arriflex IIC. Like the 200, it weighs just thirty-two pounds including camera, magazine, and lens. *Doggicam Systems***

Opposite Bottom: **When rough terrain or open water makes the use of wheeled tracking vehicles difficult or impossible, the Bickair Cable Cam delivers smooth tracking shots. The system, originally designed for shooting chase scenes in the Bond movie *Die Another Day*, can be suspended between cranes or scaffolding and uses a remote-controlled camera mount. *Bickers Action***

CHAPTER 7
PLAYING ROUGH

Stunt performers live life on the edge, striving for perfection but risking their necks every time they set off for work. Without them, none of the greatest car chases could ever have happened.

"I joined the Parachute Regiment in 1970 and became a champion recruit, but seventeen months later I had three impacted vertebrae in my lower back. Now I was a twenty-two-year-old ex-gymnastic champion, ex-armorer, and ex-para. What on earth was I going to do with my life?"

—Jim Dowdall, Stunt Coordinator, 2004

The following account is fictional, but is based on real events.

The alarm clock goes off at 5:00 a.m., the start of just another day at the office. Frank wakes with a groan. It's already been a hard week, but he rolls out of bed. He takes a quick shower before heading downstairs for a light breakfast of toast, cereal, coffee, and orange juice. Half an hour later it's time to get moving but not before checking his gear bag for the last time. It's one of those North Face jobs, tough, no nonsense, lots of room, and it hasn't fallen to pieces on him yet like so many of the others he's had in the past. He rummages through the contents but it's all there—a crash helmet, shin pads, and a change of clothes are all he'll need today. He tosses in a couple of bananas to keep his energy level up, picks up the cell phone, turns off the lights, and steps outside into the cold autumn air.

At the end of his driveway sits a new Volvo V70, and he experiences the rush of pleasure he always gets from a new toy. Still, he's earned it—not many people have got the judgment, nerve, and wits to do his job—and the Volvo fits the bill perfectly. It's no sports car, but this T5 version has a 2.4-liter 260-brake-horsepower engine, so "performance is adequate" as Rolls-Royce used to say. It has lots of space in the back for his gear, but the main thing is it's safe, with plenty of crash structures, side airbags, and curtain airbags. Safety is all important—that's something he learned years ago. He ponders his twenty-odd-year career for a moment as he settles into the driver's seat. There have been a few bumps and scrapes, but nothing serious.

Before a test jump, a relaxed Lee Sheward talks to Paul Bickers of Bickers Action. Note heavy protective padding around Sheward's neck. *Bickers Action*

Above: **A robust-looking pipe ramp in position. The parked car ostensibly "caus-es" the other car to roll over; when shot from behind, the parked car conceals the ramp from the camera.** *Bickers Action* Opposite: **The film crew makes final preparations for the shot.** *Bickers Action*

It's chilly, and winter's definitely on the way. Frank glances up at the few blackbirds already beginning their angry chatter before setting off in search of the day's food. He chuckles . . . he'll be doing some flying of his own today, but the landings are likely to be anything but birdlike. Frank's a stuntman, and in four hours he'll strap himself into a specially prepared car and aim it at a pipe ramp three hundred yards away.

Accelerating hard to his precise target speed, he'll concentrate on the line. Do it right and the front right-hand suspension of the car will connect with the angled tube of the ramp, throwing it high into the air at an angle of around 30 degrees and rolling to the left as it goes. With a bit of luck, the car should rotate through about 90 degrees before crashing down with a splintering crash and grinding of tortured metal.

There'll be a lot of sparks, but Frank knows from years of experience that there'll be little risk of fire because the small aluminum tank mounted inside the car will carry only enough fuel to complete the stunt. Also, just as the car stops moving, he will reach out to the specially fitted battery isolator switch, killing all electrical power in the car to minimize the chance of fire.

Sparks fly as Sheward connects with the ramp at speed . . . *Bickers Action*

The damaged car will still end up as a steaming heap of twisted wreckage. The stunt coordinator has specified a half roll cage to surround Frank's body in a rigid safety cell, so the rear corner of the roof will collapse like tissue paper as it slams into the tarmac, making a real mess of the shell and looking on film as though no one could have survived. The pipe ramp will be hidden in the shot by a fruit and vegetable stand conjured up by special effects, and the whole thing should look great. Frank can't wait.

The drive to Pinewood Studios takes about forty-five minutes and includes a stretch of London's notorious orbital motorway, the M25. Watching people tailgating sets Frank's teeth on edge; the average motorist has terrifyingly poor risk assessment, and they don't have the precision driving experience he has. But there's nothing much on the roads at this time of the morning, so that's good. The

. . . and takes to the skies. *Bickers Action*

Volvo's heating system has warmed up nicely, an early-morning radio show pumps out some background music, and Frank lets his mind wander over the job one more time to make sure he hasn't missed anything.

Fast forward five hours. The shoot's running a little late because of some last-minute set changes called for by the director, and Frank's been ready to go for the last hour. He's checked the car over four times since he arrived at the studio, and everything is spot on. Can't take any chances. All it takes is a bit of body rot in the wrong place, and the roll cage will punch its way through the floor when he lands, leaving the roof free to implode onto his head and arms. It happened to him once and he was lucky to get away with all fingers intact.

Some of his mates prefer not to wear full-harness seat belts, opting for a single lap strap so they can let go of the wheel, throw themselves across the passenger

Above: **Ouch! That's torn it!** *Bickers Action* Opposite Top: **Take a deep breath, it's not over yet.** *Bickers Action* Opposite Bottom: **Just one more time . . .**
Bickers Action

seat, and hold on for dear life at the moment of impact. But Frank prefers to wear a four-point harness holding him tight to the seat and put his faith in the cage—and the floor. Today he is completely confident. The car's been prepared by people he knows well, and they've added large steel plates under the mounting points of the cage to spread the load. Everything will be just fine.

At last, one of the crew gives him the nod, and the team helps him strap into the car. With his helmet tight and shin pads on to protect his legs in case they flail about in the crash, Frank fires up the engine and pulls up to the start point. He sits and lets the engine idle quietly while he collects his thoughts. He's in a world of his own now, the helmet reducing the clatter and chatter around him to a dull, muted murmur. A familiar feeling of unreality comes over him, but he also feels acutely aware of every tiny detail. He can hear the sound of his pulse beating in his throat.

Frank's mouth is a little dry, but he's not afraid for his safety; as usual he's simply anxious to do a good job and getting it right is all that matters. Without realizing it, he starts blinking a lot. He knows he always does that in the last few seconds before

Opposite Top: **Job done!** *Bickers Action*
Opposite Bottom: **The cockpit stayed remark-ably intact thanks to the substantial roll cage.** *Bickers Action* Right: **A heavily padded Lee Sheward, still smiling after just another day at the office.** *Bickers Action*

a stunt, because it was caught on in-car lipstick cameras once when he was making a documentary. According to one of the psychologists involved on the film, it's something to do with the brain wanting to take in as much data as possible when faced with a potentially dangerous event. But it's funny how the blinking stops as soon as he gets the signal to go.

And that signal comes now. He declutches, selects first gear, and floors the accelerator quickly; the engine howls in protest as he takes second gear and makes his target speed. He doesn't select third, better to let the engine scream to make the car sound as though it's going faster than it is. The pipe ramp is approaching, his heart rate has climbed to 170 but he feels calm. His body is flooded with adrenalin, but it doesn't cloud his judgment; instead, he finds it gives him a height-ened sense of awareness. His mind goes into overdrive and what happens next appears almost as if in slow motion.

As the fruit cart fills the windshield, Frank can see the pipe ramp clearly even though the carefully positioned cameras cannot. There are several cameras recording in real time and others at high speed to provide the slow-motion flashes that will be stitched into the sequence during editing. The car is equipped with lipstick cameras too, giving a driver's eye view of the action.

There's a grinding crash as suspension and ramp connect, flinging the car upward. Frank's head is driven down onto the vertebrae of his neck, and he lets out an involuntary grunt as the car launches and jinks sharply to the left in a barrel roll, jerking his head to the right. Through the windshield the world revolves like a video game, but the harness does its job and holds Frank tight in the seat. His lower legs are being knocked around a bit, but he doesn't notice and the bruises will appear later as if by magic. A nanosecond before the car's roof crashes into the tarmac, his eye catches the paramedics standing by at the end of the set. Hope we won't need them today but, ouch! That's a hard one!

Modern laminated windshields don't shatter like tempered glass, but this one does, showering Frank with a thousand tiny chunks. The windshield is just candy glass—a lollipop concoction of sugar, corn syrup, and water that breaks safely—but the impact still jars every bone in his body, forcing another involuntary grunt from between gritted teeth just before the rear section of the roof buckles down onto the back seat. But it's not over yet.

The car slides along the ground, dissipating kinetic energy in a shower of sparks and a horrendous grinding of metal. As it finally stops, Frank reaches out, flicking the battery isolator switch, killing the engine. Everything goes quiet in Frank's world save for the gentle hissing of escaping steam from a smashed radiator. Then the cheering and whooping crew arrives, and it's time to return to reality. The boys haul him out of the wreckage and he takes a few deep breaths; seconds later an immense rush hits his body like a steam train. Nothing can beat that overdose of exhilaration that follows a successful stunt, and he will be on a high for at least the next hour or so. Everything went off perfectly, the director's happy, and it's all over. Until the next time, that is.

This day in the life of stuntman Frank may be a work of fiction, but it's based on an interview with leading British stuntmen Lee Sheward and Jim Dowdall as they talked about their work and especially their attitude to safety and preparation.

Sheward has a long career stretching back to the *Doctor Who* TV series in 1963 and including movie work in *Mission: Impossible*, *Tomorrow Never Dies*, *The World Is Not Enough*, *Sahara*, and *The Bourne Supremacy* (2004). Dowdall is one of the most celebrated stuntmen and stunt coordinators in the business, with a thirty-five-year career working on major action titles such as *The Eagle Has Landed* (1976), *Superman: The Movie, Superman II* (1980), *The Long Good Friday* (1980), *Indiana Jones and the Last Crusade* (1989), *The English Patient* (1996), *Saving Private Ryan* (1998), *The 51st State*, *The Bourne Supremacy*—the list goes on and on.

Stunt performers tend to fall into two categories: those whose families fully approve of their chosen career, and those whose families would rather they had opted for a "proper job." Sheward's family is behind him, but Dowdall's family puts him in the latter category. Dowdall believes his mother never forgave him for leaving school as a gymnastics champion (but with few academic qualifications) to join the circus.

What followed is the stuff of a film script. In the circus, Dowdall was put to work assisting a German lion trainer and working as a trapeze artist. After that, he worked for a motorcycle dealer in London, then a car rental firm. He had no license but, surprisingly, began to learn the art of precision driving. One of his jobs was to park cars in spaces that were so confined he would then have to scramble out through a window.

Jim Dowdall on the set of the 1980s British TV series *Bergerac*. "When I was slim, trim, taut, and terrific," he recalls. *Jim Dowdall*

What he couldn't afford to do was scratch so much as a wing mirror, otherwise the cost of the damage would be deducted from his meager paycheck of £8 ($14) per week.

It was good experience for Dowdall but a new opportunity beckoned. His sister was a picture researcher at a London publishing company and had regular contact with a gun manufacturer supplying firearms to the film industry. Thanks to his sister, eighteen-year-old Jim Dowdall soon found himself working for the gun manufacturer. It was a dream job, with a lot of work on movie sets with stuntmen. Apart from the weapons, the company had an extensive collection of British, German, and American vehicles, including motorcycles, armored cars, Kettenkrad half-track motorcycles, and fully tracked vehicles.

In 1970 Dowdall joined the British Army, Parachute Regiment, and seventeen months later had his fateful accident, receiving three impacted vertebrae in his spine. What was a former gymnast and former para who'd worked with stunt people to do? Dowdall decided to try his luck in the film business and started doing some work as an extra to gain an Equity card. Just about that time, in 1973, Equity started the formation of the stunt register, which would define stunt performing as a distinct part of the industry. Eventually the register became very tightly regulated and the envy of the rest of the world.

Dowdall worked on *A Bridge Too Far* (1977) and the *Superman* movies, damaging another two vertebrae in his neck in the process. His precision driving career began by making safety information films for the British Government's Central Office of Information. Driving work came pouring in, and Dowdall learned to drive accurately enough to put the nose of a car within inches of a tracking vehicle–mounted camera lens. One job even involved driving an Austin Metro up the steps of a lighthouse. To make it possible, the car had an extra engine fitted in the rear to give it four-wheel drive. It was extremely crude, and Dowdall had to control the throttle of the second engine separately with a motorcycle twist grip.

The earliest car chases Dowdall remembers being involved in were *Underworld* (1985) and *Bellman and True* (1987), where Dowdall played the getaway driver in an old Jaguar. Earlier still, a bike chase in *Hanover Street* (1979) broke new ground using Panavision's answer to the Steadicam, the Panaglide. The team built a cabinet containing both camera and cameraman, which was fitted to the front of a Range Rover. The scene, believes Dowdall, broke new ground as it was shot completely on the move with no static footage.

Dozens of major feature films followed, but one of the most memorable is also one of the most recent. Dowdall describes *The Bourne Supremacy* as one of the "hairiest" chases he ever worked on, dispelling any notion that modern chases rely only on special effects and clever editing of low-speed action. Filmed in Moscow, four drivers were sent from the United Kingdom to drive all the near-miss sequences. In one scene, a Mercedes gets it wrong and powerslides across the road then gets sideswiped by a truck driven by Dowdall. The shooting continued for over a month and Dowdall reckons more car crashes were filmed during that time than you would normally expect to perform in a year.

Some German special effects guys who Dowdall had worked with before prepared four taxis (Bourne steals a taxi in the film), two of which had high-performance engines. Special equipment included a trailer hung with sprung plates to protect it from the impact of vehicles sliding into it. The star, Matt Damon, was filmed in the studio sitting in a static car being jerked by nitrogen rams to give the

Jim Dowdall prepares to double for Brosnan in *Die Another Day*. "I find my resemblance to Pierce almost uncanny once I have the wig on," says Jim. *Jim Dowdall*

impression of an impact. When the action footage and studio footage are combined, Matt Damon appears to be drilled by a police car piling into the side of his car. The work also involved extensive high-speed action filmed from a 7-liter Chevrolet pickup tracking vehicle.

The Russian stunt drivers did not speak English, so communication was tricky. After rehearsal, the Russian stuntman would drive the tracking vehicle absolutely flat out with the subject cars in hot pursuit. Action unit director Dan Bradley was keen to shoot footage for real at high speed, and Dowdall recalls that the closing impact speeds could reach 70 to 75 miles per hour compared to a more usual 20 to 25 miles per hour.

So what does it feel like sitting in the car preparing for a stunt? Dowdall says he reaches such a state of physical awareness that he feels he could turn on the switches in the car without even touching them. And like our fictitious character Frank, he feels no fear, just a sense of trepidation that something could go wrong and spoil the job. It's a risky business and despite every possible effort being made to avoid them, accidents do occasionally happen. But if either Dowdall or Sheward had their time again, would they make the same life decisions? The answer to that question from both men is unequivocal. Neither would have it any other way.

CHAPTER 8
THE TOP TWENTY

The great thing about writing a book on car chases is that friends and colleagues can argue with you all they like, but when it comes to the final cut, I get to choose the twenty car chases that have impressed me most. Let's face it, liking a film—or not—is an entirely personal thing and no two people would arrive at the same conclusion. But in this chapter I give you those films that I think are worthy of being so judged, and I explain why. You may not agree with all the choices, but even if you don't the chances are you won't get too far through this list before you have to make a beeline to the DVD store.

20. *THUNDER ROAD*

Year: 1958
Director: Arthur Ripley
Second Unit Director: Arthur Ripley
Cinematography: David Ettenson, Alan Stenswold
Stunt Coordinators: Carey Loftin, Dale Van Sickel

After the first few scenes, you might wonder how *Thunder Road* made it into this Top Twenty. But stick with it because this is an absolute classic, proving once again that there's more to car chasing than fast action and fancy editing. From a storyline by the film's star, Robert Mitchum, who had wanted for years to make a movie about running moonshine, *Thunder Road* treats us to some outstanding black-and-white footage.

Set in Kentucky, *Thunder Road* tells the story of moonshine runner Lucas Doolin (Robert Mitchum), who left the army with a glowing record to return to the family business of making and running hooch. The community has been at it for generations and is used to dodging agents of the U.S. Treasury, represented on this occasion by Troy Barrett (Gene Barry). But things become much tougher when mobster Carl Kogan (Jacques Aubuchon) muscles in to take over all the family businesses in the area. Kogan is pulling no punches, and one after another the young drivers meet their grisly end at the hands of his villainous henchmen.

D.R.M. Productions/RGA

Doolin finds himself between a rock and a hard place—law enforcement agents on one hand and Kogan's gangsters on the other. To make things worse, kid brother Robin (woodenly played by Mitchum's kid brother, James Mitchum) is hell bent on becoming a driver too. The cars are said to have been provided for the film by genuine moonshiners, and Doolin used two: a 1950 Ford Coupe "with a racing mill under the hood" and, towards the end of the film, a tuned Ford Fairlane, which Doolin informs us is "guaranteed to do a hundred and thirty on the flat." The cars were all fitted with tanks carrying 250 gallons of moonshine at a time and able to dump the lot on the road through a trick valve should the driver find himself cornered. The Ford Coupe also had an additional tank that dispensed oil onto the road from the rear, severely ruining the day of any pursuer.

Some of the acting is dire, but there are some great lines, such as "We've got mills that'll blow that heap of yours right off the road," and the storyline remains compelling. *Thunder Road* also provides a great example of early filmmaking techniques when in-car shots were filmed unconvincingly in front of a projection screen back at the studio. Watch this and then *Bullitt*, to find out how Peter Yates moved things on. Nevertheless, *Thunder Road* became a cult movie, hanging around the southern theater circuits for years after its release. Don't miss it.

19. TERMINATOR 2: JUDGMENT DAY

Year: 1991
Director: James Cameron
Second Unit Director: Gary Davies
Cinematography: Adam Greenberg
Stunt Coordinator: Gary Davies

OK, so malicious intent sets the scene for the best chases, but the sight of a boy on a trail bike being pursued by a psychopathic robot in a Freightliner truck moves that thought to an altogether new level. The boy is, of course, John Connor (Edward Furlong), who will one day grow up and fail to save the world from nuclear holocaust—as we discover in *Terminator 3: Rise of the Machines* (2003). In the original, *The Terminator*, Arnold Schwarzenegger plays a T800 Model 1 Terminator sent back in time by the Skynet, a computer system that has conquered the world, to snuff out Sarah Connor. Why? Connor's future son John will eventually become leader of the surviving humans. Thank goodness he did, because otherwise the world would not have been blessed with such classic examples of the thespian's art as "I'll be back" or "Hasta la vista, baby."

In *T2*, the T800 becomes Connor's protector against a superior T1000 machine (Robert Patrick) sent to do something unspeakable to the defenseless young John.

20th Century Fox/RGA

The T1000 is constructed from liquid metal and can reform when bits are blown off him by Arnold's armory of pump-action shotguns. But it's the combination of Patrick's slightly protruding ears and mirrored sunglasses that somehow conspire to make him even more menacing, and what follows becomes the stuff of movie legend. The entire film is a chase of one sort or another, but the one we're interested in kicks off when the T1000 catches up with Connor, who flees on his motorcycle.

The bike is especially intriguing because it has an infinite number of gears, judging by the amount of shifting going on. But watching the rebellious adolescent being hunted down relentlessly by liquid man in his sinister black truck is convincing enough to make up for such minor discrepancies. When it looks as though Connor has escaped along an L.A. storm drain we heave a sigh of relief, but it's short lived as the truck crashes down from a bridge into the concrete tract in one of the most spectacular moments of action film we'll probably ever see.

Help is at hand in the shape of the T800 riding a borrowed Harley like a true pro, scooping the young Connor on board at the last moment, then terminating the chase by duping the T1000 into a fiery collision with a bridge support. Ouch! The conflagration doesn't stop the nasty mechanical doll though, who won't take no for an answer and continues to take lethal swipes at the young man for the remainder of the film—not bad for a reject from a thermometer factory.

18. *THE ROCK*

Year: 1996
Director: Michael Bay
Second Unit Director: Michael Bay
Cinematography: John Schwartzman
Stunt Coordinator: Ken Bates

It's a no-holds-barred chase in this thriller about a mad general who takes over Alcatraz and threatens to bombard the San Francisco Bay area with missiles containing a deadly nerve gas. Our two heroes are John Patrick Mason (Sean Connery), a convicted felon who had been incarcerated in Alcatraz, and FBI chemical weapons expert Dr. Stanley Goodspeed (Nicolas Cage).

Mason decides he doesn't want to cooperate, so he creates a diversion by throwing Goodspeed's boss off the top story of a skyscraper—although attached by a thin line. After commandeering a Humvee, he escapes through the streets of San Francisco with Goodspeed following in a Ferrari F355 Spyder. The action is spectacular, with the most being made of the Humvee's size and strength when it drives straight through a truck carrying mineral water, creating quite a splash. There are plenty of classic scenes of the Humvee, Ferrari, and pursuing police cars leaping San Francisco's hills and some great long shots of the Humvee being thrown around by the stunt driver in lurid four-wheel drifts.

Don Simpson/Jerry Bruckheimer Films/Hollywood Pictures/RGA

Edited into the scene are shots of a cable-car driver entertaining his passengers in that inimitable style, and tension mounts as you await the inevitable. The Humvee continues its destructive progress, charging through cars, road works, and obstacles like a giant rampaging bull. The cable car becomes derailed when the two meet, sliding helplessly down the hill, crashing into parked cars and being blown high into the air by the ensuing conflagration. It lands and continues the slide towards the stationary Ferrari, in which Goodspeed is trapped by the airbag.

His escape provides one of the many comedic moments in the chase, along with the owner of the Humvee calling on the car phone to complain about the theft. The photography is dazzling, with lots of jerky handheld shots sucking you into the action. Minor gaffs include studio insert shots of Cage handling the Ferrari's wheel like that of a truck, an old lady crossing in front of the Humvee who doesn't look a day over twenty-five even with the wig, and some of the corny jokes. As a piece of footage though, it's superb, only lacking sinister intent for a top-of-the-league ranking.

17. *TO LIVE AND DIE IN L.A.*

Year: 1985
Director: William Friedkin
Second Unit Director: Buddy Joe Hooker
Cinematography: Robert D. Yeoman
Stunt Coordinator: Buddy Joe Hooker

New Century Productions/RGA

Reviewers are undecided about this revenge film, but stuntman Dick Ziker nevertheless won two Stuntman Awards for *To Live and Die in L.A.*, one of them for "best vehicular stunt" and one for "most spectacular sequence." The plot follows the tale of secret service agent Richard Chance (William L. Petersen), whose partner and mentor is murdered by ruthless counterfeiter, Eric Masters (Willem Dafoe).

Friedkin, remember, directed *The French Connection,* in which driving legends Bill Hickman and Carey Loftin performed an unforgettable chase. In truth, the cars in this film are a little boring, and perhaps there's a lesson here in that a flock of run-of-the-mill Chevys ultimately have limited appeal no matter what you do to them. Soundwise, the chase could be better too, but visually it mixes it up, starting from an industrial site where the chasers dodge forklifts and make a slalom course out of a dozen or so large trucks.

There's some great footage of our heroes mixing it with the Santa Fe Railroad while being shot at by the bad guys from the other side of the tracks. They escape along the L.A. storm drain—of course—only to be set upon by more protagonists coming at them from every direction.

The climax of the scene is probably one of the earliest examples of chasing into oncoming traffic as the noose draws tighter. Maybe this is the clip the judges had in mind when giving the award to Ziker, because the variety of angles—both high- and low-level, in-car, and from static camera positions—make for a gripping and memorable sequence. The dialogue is apt to be a little canned and some of the acting wooden, but during the chase you feel the fear of the two targets, and for a minute there, it looked as though there was going to be no escape.

16. *THE MATRIX RELOADED*

Year: 2003
Directors: The Wachowski Brothers
Second Unit Director: David Ellis
Cinematography: Bill Pope
Stunt Coordinator: R. A. Rondell (driving)

Was there ever a more unlikely movie in which to find a car chase sequence? There is some pretty amazing action, however, which is a relief from the exhausting task of trying to understand the usual ludicrous *Matrix* plot. Early scenes on the custom-built freeway are impressive, and you would be hard pressed to guess it isn't for real. A good deal of the footage is though, particularly the shots of cars being hit from behind by others which then shoot up in the air and roll into oblivion thanks to traveling pipe ramps.

There's some horrific stuff, such as the SUV being machine-gunned and rolling to destruction. In fact, a lot of cars roll to destruction in this movie, and it all gets

General Motors

fairly grim. Of all the favorite approaches to chases that seem to be emerging these days, especially after *Ronin*, the idea of driving against the traffic seems to be the most popular. This time thrills were courtesy of Trinity, played by Carrie-Anne Moss, who did some of the easier driving herself, and especially stuntwoman Debbie Evans, whose amazing riding coupled with carefully chosen camera angles emphasized the speed and produced breathtaking footage. This is one of those sequences where your brain quickly rationalizes that what you are watching is impossible, but you are nevertheless shocked at every swerve.

Many of the basic ingredients for a great chase were in this one, almost like someone had consulted a recipe: the speed, the close shaves, crushing against walls, and so on. But it still placed a little too much reliance on mass destruction, almost as if the filmmakers lacked confidence in their ability to deliver by making do with terrifying near misses. The press releases say hundreds of cars were destroyed during the movie's making. The cost of highway was $30 million. Compared to something like *Bullitt,* which was shot with four main cars in two weeks on public roads, it seems the movie industry is ready and willing to splash huge expenses, which aren't always reflected in the end result. The concrete runway of *The Matrix Reloaded* was desperately one-dimensional however many cars were wrecked.

That said, it's still an amazing spectacle that relied heavily on genuine stunts for most of the action, with the major special effects being saved for the crumpling truck at the end of the scene. It makes it to my Top Twenty, but definitely falls into the category of those chases that rely on gratuitous panel bashing rather than emphasizing driving skills. And if you like cars a lot, that can be tough to take.

15. *THE FRENCH CONNECTION*

Year: 1971
Director: William Friedkin
Second Unit Director: William Friedkin
Cinematography: Owen Roizman
Stunt Coordinator: Bill Hickman

Featuring mostly real high-speed driving, the tension is visceral as Popeye Doyle (Gene Hackman) pursues an elevated electric train across twenty-six blocks of Brooklyn. Again, it's the reality that makes this sequence so compelling. It starts with the despair in the voice and body language of the Pontiac Le Mans' owner as he's dragged from the driver's seat. He stands there watching his rear tires go up in smoke as Doyle kicks off with a monster U-turn, and it's clear he doesn't expect to see his prized possession again. But then, he wouldn't want to when Doyle has finished with it.

The chase is a combination of near misses and hits filmed partly in-car and partly using exterior shots to bring us to the edge of our seats. During the desperate journey,

20th Century Fox/RGA

Doyle redefines road rage, shouting and pounding at the wheel whenever a car crosses his path and becoming apoplectic whenever his own mistakes slow him down still further. What makes this chase so original is the fact that Doyle isn't portrayed as an expert driver but simply a rather clumsy cop in a big hurry. With the amount of damage Doyle inflicts on the Pontiac, it's hard to imagine there's a straight panel left on the smoldering wreck once the rampage is over.

Onboard the train, meanwhile, the Frenchman sticks up the driver, ordering him to miss the next station. Doyle, already panting with exertion from the driving, has stopped by now and sprinted up the stairs to the platform without result. By the time he gets back to the car, his frustration is palpable, the tension rising to a fever pitch as he continues the pursuit. The success of the sequence is as much due to Hackman's Oscar-winning performance as the action itself. The most compelling car chases must succeed on the primitive level of the hunter closing in on its quarry, and we are left with absolutely no doubt as to what Doyle's intentions are once he catches up with his.

14. *DIE ANOTHER DAY*

Year: 2002
Director: Lee Tamahori
Second Unit Director: Vic Armstrong
Cinematography: David Tattersall
Stunt Coordinators: Vic Armstrong, G. A. Aguilar

Bond movies in general should almost get the number-one spot considering the number of fantastic sequences involving cars the franchise has delivered over the years. There was the fabulous Aston Martin DB5 in *Goldfinger* and again in *Thunderball*; the Toyota 2000GT in *You Only Live Twice*; the flying AMC Hornet in *The Man with the Golden Gun*; a Lotus Esprit in *The Spy Who Loved Me*; another Lotus Esprit, this time a Turbo version, in *For Your Eyes Only*; an Aston Martin DBS and Vantage in *The Living Daylights*; a BMW Z3 in *GoldenEye*; a BMW 7-Series in

Aston Martin

Tomorrow Never Dies; and a BMW Z8 in *The World Is Not Enough*. Interlaced with that lot are various other cars used to spoil Bond's day.

Then, in *Die Another Day*, Bond lands back in an Aston at last, this time a Vanquish. On a frozen lake, he discovers that a Jaguar XKR convertible equipped with an optional Gatling gun can be something of a nuisance, and a formidable battle ensues between the two. In reality, the lake was fragile enough for cars to be equipped with flotation bags in case the surface gave way, and one stunt driver was concussed in a collision with an iceberg; they don't come any more real than that, despite the over-the-top CGI used in some other scenes.

Action unit director Vic Armstrong concocted some great sequences during the chase, all well edited and dovetailing perfectly with some of the Ice Palace scenes shot back in the United Kingdom. Over the years we've been treated to some great stuff, but what makes Bond chases so compelling? Like Bond himself, the chases are a mixture of fun and a degree of deadly intent, which get us on the edge of our seats. They are also on the cutting edge technically too, so we can always look forward to what's coming in the next one. More of the same, please.

13. *TAXI/TAXI 2*
Year: 1998/2000
Director: Gérard Pirès/Gérard Krawczyk
Second Unit Director: Gérard Pirès/Robert Kechichian
Cinematography: Jean-Pierre Sauvaire/Gérard Sterin
Stunt Coordinator: Michel Julienne/Rémy Julienne

It's been said elsewhere in this Top Twenty that the most compelling chases are those with serious intent and where the chase, if you like, is a chase to the death. But there are always exceptions to the rule, and *Taxi* (the 1998 original and not the 2004 U.S. remake) is one. Written and produced by Luc Besson, once known as a director of well-made car commercials, *Taxi* plays for laughs, some wicked Gallic humor coming across loud and clear even through the subtitles.

The plot is simple enough and that's great because you can concentrate on laughing out loud and being wowed by the chase sequences coordinated by Rémy Julienne's son, Michel. Daniel (Samy Naceri), a pizza delivery boy, who can beat any of his mates against the clock on a scooter, turns taxi driver. But this is no conventional taxi. An array of switches in the glove box raises the Peugeot 406 on pneumatic jacks, unfolds huge front and rear spoilers, widens the wheel track by a foot, leaving Daniel simply to unclip the Peugeot steering wheel and replace it with a three-spoke Momo.

The film opens with a low following shot of Daniel on his scooter attempting to break the crosstown record in a breathtaking display of riding. But we soon move on

Le Studio Canal+/RGA

to four wheels and a scene where Daniel picks up a passenger who, late for the airport, makes the mistake of telling Daniel to get a move on. Michel Julienne does a superb and inventive job with the chase choreography, and there's more, much more, as the film progresses.

The law soon catches up with Daniel, and he is pressed into service to help apprehend some German bank robbers driving a pair of unmarked AMG Mercedes (only AMG versions smoke tires at 50 miles per hour). The final chase is truly spectacular, and you'll still be laughing your head off when it comes.

Taxi 2 was made soon after the original and once more featured Daniel and his 406, which now has folding wings to aid longer leaps. The opening scene once again goes straight into a drive sequence, this time riding with Jean-Louis Schlesser in a Peugeot World Rally Car. It's not hard to guess what happens next. Daniel's taxi appears in the rear-view mirror en route to the hospital carrying an expectant mother. There are plenty more laughs, and with Japanese bad guys driving Mitsubishi Evo VIs, replacing the German villains in Mercs, the pace is even more frantic. Stunts are this time coordinated by the great man himself, Rémy Julienne. Watch out for the hilarious ending of the final chase when an optimistic villain realizes his automatic pistol is no substitute for an 88mm tank gun.

20th Century Fox/RGA

12. *VANISHING POINT*

Year: 1971
Director: Richard C. Sarafian
Second Unit Director: Richard C. Sarafian
Cinematography: John A. Alonzo
Stunt Coordinator: Carey Loftin

Did he? Well, did he? Did Kowalski mean to end it all or not? Was this a miscalculation by the man we've watched making perfect judgments for the last hour and a half, or had he just had enough? *Vanishing Point* stars Barry Newman as the troubled hero whose flashbacks reveal the sad tale of a life in turmoil and memories of events he'd rather forget. His mission is to drive a Challenger R/T from Denver to San Francisco in fifteen hours for a bet.

He soon picks up a tail in the form of a couple of highway patrol motorcycles, and the trouble starts when Kowalski forces the unfortunate bikers into a ditch. We learn of our hero's underlying tender nature at this point when the first flashback reveals a young Kowalski suffering a particularly nasty dirt bike race smash. Back in the now, Kowalski pauses to make sure the prone policeman is OK, and then disappears in a cloud of tire smoke. Kowalski may be soft but the police are not, and the chase steadily escalates, egged on by blind DJ "Super Soul" who backs the rebel Kowalski's cause.

To be honest, the entire story is crazy, Kowalski making a rod for his own back that grows more unyielding as the chase progresses. On his way, he meets an eccentric hippie in a beaten-up Series One E-Type Jag who wants to race (losing, big time), a prospector in the middle of the Mojave Desert, and a snake charmer. But just when you think things couldn't get any more bizarre, he comes across a naked woman riding a Honda motorcycle.

But the driving is one long V-8–fest of splendid action thanks to the great Carey Loftin's superb stunt coordination. So too is the photography, with endless and spectacular long shots of the white Challenger, storming across miles of dead-straight desert roads. It all ends in tears, of course. Kowalski finally gives due consideration to whether he can barge his way through a roadblock comprising the two most famous Caterpillar bulldozers ever filmed and dies in the attempt. Or does he? Surely there's a sequel waiting to be made? We demand to be told!

11. *GONE IN 60 SECONDS*

Year: 1974
Director: H. B. Halicki
Second Unit Director: H. B. Halicki
Cinematography: Scott Lloyd-Davies, Jack Vacek
Stunt Coordinator: H. B. Halicki

H. B. Halicki/RGA

The granddaddy of car chases in many respects, the main chase at the end of this movie is also probably the longest. The film is made all the more remarkable by the fact that the original *Gone* was also largely an amateur production, written, produced, and directed by H.B. Halicki, a wealthy businessman and car nut. Halicki also does the driving in the film's legendary star, the 1973 Mustang, Eleanor, as well as coordinating the sequences. He does a good job, and much of the work is clearly filmed at high speed, Halicki demonstrating fine car control while taking out a sizable quantity of other cars that makes *The Matrix Reloaded* look like a low-budget production.

In-car footage has an unsanitized feel similar to that of *Bullitt*, the camera vibrating vigorously enough to create an unusually vivid feel. The soundtrack is a thriller too, although the softer throb of the later V-8 lacks the intimidating, metallic harshness of McQueen's Mustang GT. The pursuit takes place around the Los Angeles, Redondo Beach, and Long Beach areas on city streets and highways as well as an off-road dusty wasteland where some of the cleverest shots are filmed. More than the average amount of destruction takes place in the movie generally, and car lovers will weep at several Mopar classics that get crunched, cars that would today command handsome prices among collectors.

The driving and stunts are great, and it's a shame that Halicki didn't stick to the driving and hire some writers to give the plot some pace and clarity. That said, had *Gone* been produced to that level of quality, we may never have been given the Jerry Bruckheimer remake. After all, no one has attempted a remake of *Bullitt*, now have they?

Year: 2000
Director: Dominic Sena
Second Unit Director: Phillip C. Pfeiffer
Cinematography: Paul Cameron
Stunt Coordinators: Johnny Martin, Chuck Picerni Jr., John Hugh McKnight, Bill Young (Precision Driving Team coordinators)

The remake and the original are impossible to separate because both feature chases that are equally worthy in completely different ways. Everything about the original needed major editing, and it's arguable that even the car sequences overstayed their welcome. The later full-on Hollywood production exhibited all the major filmmaking skills you would expect, so the pace is fast, grabs the attention, and refuses to let go.

This time there's a lot more "Grand Theft Auto" than pursuit going on, but when it comes the chase is a good one. Nicolas Cage as Memphis Raines does a conspic-

Touchstone Pictures/RGA

uously good job behind the wheel in several of the in-car sequences. Expert manipulation of the light yields some glorious shots during the chase with subtle colors and glistening road surfaces adding to the atmosphere. And then there's the car. This time, Eleanor is a 1967 Shelby Mustang, specially created for the picture, complete with a number of customized body features.

When the inevitable L.A. storm drains (what would Hollywood do without them?) enter the chase, great aerial views from the chasing helicopter lend a new feel to this familiar choice of location. Lots of long-lens shots emphasize Eleanor's steroidal looks and ultra-low ground clearance, generating plenty of excitement by the time we get to the big jump.

Actually, it's probably one of the best jumps ever filmed and shown in several stages as it develops, some clips in real time and some in slow-mo. Coolest of all is the in-car shot through the windshield as the car is landing. You can believe it's genuine; just look at how the stunt driver has remembered to avoid injury by keeping his thumbs over the top of the wheel rim alongside his fingers, rather than hooking his thumb beneath the rim.

There are some great lines in the movie as well, plus a satisfying ending for a change. And for once, this cover version has greatly improved upon the execution of the original, even if the driving pretty much breaks even.

RastarPictures/Universal Pictures/RGA

10. SMOKEY AND THE BANDIT

Year: 1977
Director: Hal Needham
Second Unit Director: Alan Gibbs
Cinematography: Bobby Byrne
Stunt Coordinator: Stan Barrett

One of the most widely listed among the top car chase films, but in some ways also one of the least likely. Is this really a car chase movie, or a kind of extended romp with the good ol' boys down south? A bit of both, perhaps. The chases are certainly just that, with bootlegger Bandit (Burt Reynolds) doing his best to evade Smokey in the form of various police chiefs and one in particular—Sheriff Buford T. Justice. Bandit's chosen weapon is that 1970s classic, a Pontiac Trans Am, whose opened-up pipes give us a treat every time he hits the gas pedal. There are V-8 engines and V-8 engines, but the sound of this one combines that kind of good-natured baritone waffle with a wolverine howl when opened up that makes hairs stand up on the back of your neck.

There's not too much subtlety in *Smokey and the Bandit.* Although we get the odd display of close-quarters precision, most of it is highway work interlaced with plenty of off-roading—either intentional or unintentional. There are some fine head-on long shots of the Trans Am on the limit and, as always in a Burt Reynolds movie,

158

a good deal of panel bending as the cops collide with each other in their eagerness to get their man.

Bandit's good buddy, Cledus "Snowman" Snow actually hauls the booze in his Kenilworth truck, which makes an interesting counterpoint to the big Pontiac. And just as we are beginning to think the combination of truck and car in chases is just too incredible (what's the point of a fast car with a slow truck in tow?), we get the answer. Overhauled by a motorcycle cop, Snowman receives the news that he was traveling at 96 miles per hour. We wait with bated breath to see how Bandit can rescue his chum from this dilemma and are once again given the answer as the Trans Am arrives at speed and performs a perfect handbrake turn alongside. Just in case the good officer fails to be impressed by the stunt, Bandit's girlfriend, Carrie (Sally Field), delivers the one-fingered salute. That does the trick and the rest is joyous history.

Reynolds' films are infamous for the chase sequences, and several would qualify for this slot. They're spectacular good-natured fun, and they make a change from the usual city street action we get used to seeing. One visual treat in the film comes not as result of a chase, but when Snowman gets some rough treatment in a gas-station bar at the hands of some out-of-state Hells Angels. Back in the safety of the Kenilworth's driving seat, a broad grin crosses his battered face. His assailants' bikes are parked at the other end of the lot. You can imagine the rest.

9. *THE BLUES BROTHERS*

Year: 1980
Director: John Landis
Second Unit Director: John Landis
Cinematography: Stephen M. Katz
Stunt Coordinator: Gary McLarty

"The use of unnecessary violence in the apprehension of the Blues Brothers has been approved." Well, if a hundred or so of your police cars had just been trashed, you would probably be as annoyed too. But life wasn't to get any simpler for this long-suffering police controller; he'd lose another couple of hundred before the film was over.

It goes without saying that *The Blues Brothers* is an absolute classic thanks to John Belushi (Joliet Jake Blues) and Dan Ackroyd (Elwood Blues). But it's easy to overlook just how terrific the two major chases are when you are busy lapping up the music dished out not just by the brothers themselves, but by Aretha Franklin, Ray Charles, Cab Calloway, James Brown, and a host of other great stars. The action scenes *are* mighty good though. The first rushes us through a shopping mall with breathtaking destructive force that eventually has you averting your eyes from the screen. Somehow, you just can't stop thinking of what it would be like to clean up the mess.

Universal/RGA

The great chase at the end begins with that immortal line, "It's a hundred and six miles to Chicago, we've got a full tank of gas, half a pack of cigarettes, it's dark, and we're wearing sunglasses." But among all the humor, there's some incredibly creative stunt coordination with some amazing jumps and drifting Dodges. The horrific drop from the unfinished bridge—from a height of what looks like ten thousand feet—taken by the head Nazi (Henry Gibson) is enough to make the audience gasp in horror but still manage a snicker. The chase is endless, but even we have to shed a little tear along with Jake and Elwood when, on making their escape and parking, the trusty old Dodge sedan spontaneously falls to pieces.

The award for the best verbal exchange during a car chase also goes to *The Blues Brothers:*

> (loud bang and oil spraying on the windshield)
> Elwood: "Oh no, the motor, it's thrown a rod."
> Joliet Jake: "Is that serious?"
> Elwood: "Yup."

8. *C'ÉTAIT UN RENDEZVOUS*

Year: 1976
Director: Claude Lelouch
Second Unit Director: Claude Lelouch
Cinematography: Claude Lelouch
Stunt Coordinator: Claude Lelouch

Not a classic car chase in the true sense, but close enough. This is one of the most breathtaking pieces of film you will ever see. Less than nine minutes long, the film shows a high-speed dash across the center of Paris from a camera mounted on the front bumper. You never actually see the car the camera is fitted to, but it sounds like an early Ferrari and it's in a big hurry. The camera angle is low, over-emphasizing the speed, but what you see is genuine, the camera has not been over-cranked. *Rendezvous* opens with the banner, "Le film que vous allez voir a été réalisé sans aucun trucage ni accéléré," which effectively translates to "the film you are about to see has not been speeded up." We can believe that because Lelouch revealed all for the writing of this book and you can read the full details in Chapter 2. But the bottom line is, Lelouch did drive the car for real, he was jumping red lights, he was driving rapidly, though not at racing speeds, and he did get arrested by the authorities when the film was released. But none of that is really the point. In making *Rendezvous*, Lelouch showed what a gift he has for filmmaking. The short, intoxicating piece of footage blows your mind over and over, no matter how many times you watch it, and the great thing is, you don't have to wade through DVD scene selection to find it. *C'était Rendezvous* is a must-have in any car nut's collection.

Spirit Level Films

Kennedy Miller Productions/RGA

7. *THE ROAD WARRIOR [AKA MAD MAX 2]*

Year: 1981
Director: George Miller
Second Unit Director: Brian Hannant
Cinematography: Dean Semler
Stunt Coordinator: Max Aspin

This is undoubtedly a car chase movie, but there are plenty of other vehicles in the mix too, from bikes and trikes to supercharged pickup trucks and fuel tankers. In case you've been living on Mars for the last twenty-five years, *Mad Max* was Mel Gibson's ticket to stardom. The story is set in the Australia of the future, when civilized society is disintegrating and marauding gangs are barely kept in check by a besieged police force.

In *The Road Warrior* gasoline has become the world's most precious commodity, and there is no sign of the police. Gibson again plays "Mad" Max Rockatansky, our embittered, limping hero—a bad guy in the first film shot him in the knee—who hooks up with a band of honest folk refining fuel in the desert who are constantly besieged by bandits. The entire film is pretty well filled with vehicles and action, but there are two key chase sequences. The first is short but grabs your attention instantly.

The film opens with Max cruising along a desert road in his black Interceptor and being overhauled by bandits. Forced to kill the supercharger when he notices the fuel gauge bouncing on empty, Max finds himself quickly overwhelmed and the first bout of vehicular combat begins. The stunts are real, dangerous, violent, and exciting as Max repels invaders and sends a couple to rendezvous with that great fuel tanker in the sky.

The second and much longer chase comes towards the end when the desert community breaks out of the compound, Max heading in one direction in a battering ram–equipped Mack fuel tanker while most of the others head off in the other. The bandits chase the tanker of course and a moving pitch battle ensues with some gut-wrenching action and lethal-looking stunts clearly filmed for real. Plenty of speed, some great driving, and a fair degree of gratuitous violence make this sequence a must-see for chase lovers.

6. *THE BOURNE IDENTITY*

Year: 2002
Director: Doug Liman
Second Unit Director: Alexander Witt
Cinematography: Don Burgess, Dan Mindel, Oliver Wood
Stunt Coordinators: Martin Hub, Nick Powell

Kalimah Productions/RGA

Life is tough for Jason Bourne. After being fished out of the sea and presumed dead, a fisherman surgeon removes two bullets and a tiny laser projector containing the number of a Swiss bank account—ouch! An indignant Bourne awakens (loudly) and a tale of intrigue begins. Bourne's quest to establish his identity is constantly interfered with by CIA hit men.

The chase leads to Paris, where with love interest Marie in tow, Bourne finds himself at the end of some unwelcome attention by the gendarmerie. The car? A battered Mk II Mini complete with nasty British Leyland steering wheel, Webasto sunroof, and faded red paint. Spotted by the Feds, Bourne quietly asks Marie whether she takes care of the car and she tells him it pulls a little to the right. It's a nice touch and signals the start of some of the finest precision driving you will ever see.

The director makes maximum use of the Mini's diminutive size (you won't see this done in a Mopar) with our heroes taking to narrow alleyways and sidewalks to lose all but the police motorcyclists. The fact that Marie is scared witless by the ride adds to the authenticity, especially when Bourne announces, "We've got a bump coming up," before plunging down the inevitable stone steps. But hey, it's a Mini, it's Paris . . . what do you expect?

The Mini driver's car control is outstanding—if you want to see a perfect demonstration of tail sliding a front-wheel-drive car, then this is it. The Mini's performance is quick, tight, and precise rather than fast and wild, and after a catalog of tight squeezes, a trip the wrong way up a one-way street during rush hour whittles the number of pursuer's down to one motorcyclist. Bourne is on the sidewalk, the bike cop on the road, craning to see the Mini over the roofs of the parked cars. Unfortunately, the cop doesn't spot the Peugeot 405 pulling out in front of him and T-bones it in a spectacular and painful-looking final stunt.

The Bourne Identity certainly has one of the better chases. It is detailed, convincing, and unpredictable despite the choice of both car and location. Great external shots are mixed with well-edited in-car shots of wheelmanship, gear selection, and Marie's discomfort.

5. *LE PROFESSIONNEL*

Year: 1981
Director: Georges Lautner
Second Unit Director: N/A
Cinematography: Henri Decaë
Stunt Coordinator: N/A

Le Professionnel is one of those tongue-in-cheek secret-agent thrillers that mostly strays close to the edge of credibility and frequently steps over it. Jean-Paul

Le Studio Canal+/Author collection

Belmondo plays French agent Joss Beaumont sent by his government to assassinate a Third World dictator. Halfway through the job, though, there's a change in the political climate and Beaumont is turned in by his own side.

Captured, drugged, and interrogated, Beaumont is finally sentenced to a dismal future, breaking rocks in the blistering heat. Naturally he plans a spectacular escape and returns home, not only to reap revenge on his former bosses, but determined to knock over the dictator anyway just to prove that he can. The car chase is only three or four minutes long, and Beaumont, piloting a Fiat 131 Mirafiori with huge panache, is pursued by two heavies in a black Peugeot 504. This is a refreshingly real sequence, helped by the fact that Belmondo does his own driving and is clearly visible both in-car and through the windshield, giving the hapless 131 a severe beating.

What sets this chase apart from the rest is not just the outstanding stunt coordination and cinematography, but the way in which the hunted turns hunter thanks to a bout of road rage brought on when one of the crooks takes a potshot at Beaumont. We're not sure at this point whether our French hero is more annoyed about the flesh wound, the hole in his designer leather jacket, or just the affront to his manhood. Whatever, he sets off in relentless pursuit of the Peugeot, chasing it through narrow streets and avenues, up and down stone steps nose-to-tail, and even nose-to-nose as the crooks try to escape in reverse. By then, both cars are battered almost beyond recognition thanks to Beaumont's preference for ramming the opposition into submission.

There are some truly memorable moments in this chase, which is full of raw, hard-edged, genuine footage with apparently few special effects, not to mention some quite amazing driving captured by fine cinematography. The icing on the cake is the sound of the Fiat twin-cam 1,595cc engine at full throttle, slurping air noisily through its downdraft Weber carburetor in true thoroughbred Italian style. Great stuff.

4. *THE ITALIAN JOB*

Year: 1969
Director: Peter Collinson
Second Unit Director: Philip Wrestler
Cinematography: Douglas Slocombe
Stunt Coordinator: Rémy Julienne

Ironically, the brilliance of the action scenes in *the* 1960s classic appeal for entirely different reasons now, as perhaps they did then. Back then the performance of the three Mini Cooper S's may have been perceived as daring, but today it looks almost sedate, at times, in comparison with some of the high-speed demolition footage that has subsequently emerged. You'll notice that in this film our heroic red, white, and blue trio tiptoe down cathedral steps, zoom through a sewer, splash across the top of a weir, tear along pedestrian-packed sidewalks, and leap across the roofs of Fiat's Turin factory without suffering so much as a scratch.

What we're treated to instead is precision driving in some of the most accomplished and finest-handling cars the world has ever seen, orchestrated by possibly the greatest stunt driver in film history, Rémy Julienne. Most of the chase scenes we see in *The Italian Job* are extended rather than closely cropped; most of the performances you see happened in real time with no special effects to hide behind and no visible speeded-up footage.

The Italian Job has plenty of comedy in it, but isn't really a comic film. There's nothing funny about the Mafia, represented by Altabani (Raffaele Vallone), stamping its mark on the proceedings in the first scene by bumping off Beckerman (Rossano Brazzi) and his Lamborghini Miura in a particularly nasty way. And you just know they're not kidding when they threaten Charlie Croker (Michael Caine) on the mountain, not to mention dumping an E-Type and Aston into the abyss as well.

So in summary we've got classic cars, the world's greatest stunt drivers, and a superbly creative script unrivaled even today in the number of one-liners it spawned. Then there's the amazing scenery, the glorious soundtrack—including "On Days Like

Oakhurst Productions/Paramount Pictures/RGA

These" from Quincy Jones, Don Black, and Matt Munro—and an all-star cast, including the unforgettable Benny Hill, Irene Handl, and let's not forget Michael Caine. All these elements coalesce into a package that proves there is far more to making a memorable car chase film than the chase sequences alone. *The Italian Job* oozes 1960s style and reeks of class, but, most of all, it has immense charm. There's no doubt it's a tough act to follow and always will be.

Year: 2003
Director: F. Gary Gray
Second Unit Directors: Ken Bates, Alexander Witt
Cinematography: Wally Pfister
Stunt Coordinators: Ken Bates, Kurt Bryant, Gary Hymes, Gianluca Petrazzi

This film wouldn't make the Top Twenty on its own but is worthy of a mention alongside its classic namesake. The movie cleverly updates the original theme into a twenty-first-century version of the story without resorting to being just another clumsy remake, so for that we all give thanks. There's much less car chasing footage than in the original and ironically, the updated MINI plays less of a seminal role than the original Mini and contributes far less to the overall action. Although a leaf has

BMW GB Ltd

been taken out of the Peter Yates school of chase making with close-ups of the actors at the wheel, they handle their cars as if on their way to the supermarket, which is a poor fit with the external action shots with stunt drivers in control. It's a lesson for filmmakers aspiring to make the most compelling footage—choose stars who can drive.

There's a fair amount of dramatic license; I'd defy anyone to get a MINI away from the line with a ton and a half of gold in the back, never mind doing a hand-brake turn. And the engines of the MINIs seem to get more serious halfway through, like they've just had a power implant. The link with Turin by starting in Vienna is plausible and there are some great action scenes uniquely suited to MINIs, like the trip down the stone steps—something that would prove a lot trickier in a Dodge Charger or BMW 5-Series. The chase through the sewer is also a nice link to the original, with nose landings that'll make you wince. The idea of blowing the ground out from beneath the things you want to pinch is a great idea and so too is all the computer nerding with Napster and his 3D imaging.

Sadly, no great one-liners such as, "You were only supposed to blow the bloody doors off," or "In this country, they drive on the wrong side of the road." The humor and characterizations aren't up to the original (Michael Caine, Noel Coward, Benny Hill, and Irene Handl are a tough act to follow). But the avoidance of too much violence and gratuitous killing pays off, which just goes to show that getting bums on seats doesn't necessarily depend on an orgy of Uzis and rivers of blood.

3. *THE SEVEN-UPS*

Year: 1973
Director: Philip D'Antoni
Second Unit Director: Philip D'Antoni
Cinematography: Urs Furrer
Stunt Coordinator: Bill Hickman

Phil D'Antoni, the producer behind *Bullitt* and *The French Connection*, also produced this thriller in which Roy Scheider plays Buddy Manucci, head of the Seven-Ups, a crack squad of undercover New York cops. The squad gets its name from the sentence usually meted out to the crooks it convicts, usually seven years or more, and the plot is a convoluted mixture of bluff and double bluff as Manucci and his men attempt to trap a kidnap gang. In the process, one of the Seven-Ups (played by Ken Kercheval of *Dallas* fame) is murdered at the hands of Bo, played by legendary stunt driver Bill Hickman.

Five years after driving the black Charger in *Bullitt*, Hickman looks older and has been given a particularly bad 1970s hairdo. Nevertheless, his talents remain

20th Century Fox/RGAz

undiminished, both behind the wheel and as a coordinator of some outstanding sequences in this extended chase lasting some eight minutes. The two cars are a Pontiac Grandville driven by Hickman and a Pontiac Ventura probably driven by the other stunt driver credited for the film, Larry Summers (doubling Scheider).

What we get is a combination of city and rural, most of which is filmed car-to-car with all the gritty realism of *Bullitt*. We ride with the drivers through the streets of New York at a pace that is clearly not faked, something highlighted by Hickman's firm grasp of the steering wheel during some of the in-car footage. We may no longer be out west, but the team still manages to find some San Francisco–esque hill sections over which to jump the cars. The substitution of the Grandville for the more serious metal used in *Bullitt* makes for some spectacular action at this point; it's like watching someone trying to fly a battleship.

Interestingly, there are some remarkably familiar engine sounds coming from inside the Pontiac. On some occasions it sounds like a manual—the V-8 engine note is particularly harsh and do we hear some double declutching going on? It's particularly odd since views of the driver's feet stamping on the brake pedal show that it's every bit an automatic. Legend has it that the *Bullitt* sound-track was raided for *The Seven-Ups*.

No matter. It works, and this is one of the finest car chases ever made. Despite at least one completely inappropriate car, it mixes serious high-speed action with eyeball-wrenching photography, superb in-car shots, and great sound. Then there's that final ingredient that sets the best chases aside from the rest.

Others choose to add humor to their chases but in this one, you'll believe this is a life-and-death pursuit.

2. *RONIN*

Year: 1998
Director: John Frankenheimer
Second Unit Director: John Frankenheimer
Cinematography: Robert Fraisse
Stunt Coordinator: Jean-Claude Lagniez

Ronin is named after ancient Japanese Samurai warriors whose masters had lost their lives, leaving the Samurais to get work where they could, relieving people of their heads for a few yen here and there. Too violent? Come on, a guy has to earn a living. Anyway, the characters in the film are similar ex–Cold War guerrilla fighters or espionage agents out on a limb and left with nothing to do except cause trouble in exchange for money. This time, the unruly band of men and one woman, Deirdre (Natascha McElhone), led by Sam (Robert De Niro) are hired to retrieve a metal case containing something that everyone wants.

MGM/RGA

The whole thing turns particularly nasty, and with double-crossers double-crossing the double-crossers, at times it's quite confusing too. However, the car chase sequences in the south of France near La Turbie, and later in Paris, have been hailed as the finest ever. Indeed, the late John Frankenheimer set out to achieve just that, firing one stunt team and calling in Jean-Claude Lagniez, who in turn called in race drivers Neugarten, Lemarier, and former F1 supremo Jean-Pierre Jarier to steer the cars. With no faking of film speed and some extremely intricate editing for fast-paced action, Frankenheimer and his team deliver the ultimate in car chase stunt work that modern cinematography can deliver. Nothing filmed since (nor most things filmed before) can even come close to this spectacular piece of work.

So why doesn't it get the top spot? A number of reasons. First of all, none of the stars playing protagonists in *Ronin* were actually drivers. The in-car work was oh-so-clever, to the extent of seating the actors in front of dummy wheels in right-hand-drive cars, or with stunt drivers controlling cars from the back of the car via an extended steering column system. And although the artists' expressions regularly exhibit shock and even genuine fear (the stunt drivers' worked at between 75 and 100 miles per hour), the scenes lack the confidence of a true wheelman. In some clips, De Niro looks as though he is suffering from acute indigestion, whereas McQueen, Hickman, Belmondo in *Le Professionnel,* and even Nicolas Cage in *Gone in 60 Seconds,* all handle the wheel with the convincing skill of working hands.

As far as Lagniez' stunt work is concerned, it is arguable that some of the phenomenal sequences he and his team put together have never been equaled. As he himself says, all the work was carried out at high speed, Frankenheimer refusing to countenance anything but the real deal. But while the modern style of fast editing adds pace to the action, a stream of clips a nanosecond long can be frustrating to watch; especially if you are keen on seeing cars driven well. With all that said, *Ronin* is one of the best of the best, with brilliant and intoxicating chase scenes always ending in tears for someone. You can't ask for more than that.

1. *BULLITT*

Year: 1968
Director: Peter Yates
Second Unit Director: Peter Yates
Cinematography: William Fraker
Stunt Coordinator: Carey Loftin

It begins with the black Charger R/T sliding into view from behind a trailer. The camera cuts to a shot through the Mustang's grubby windshield and catches Frank Bullitt (Steve McQueen) sizing up the opposition and wearing that customary deadpan expression along with a classic 1960s turtleneck sweater. He reaches down and we hear the click of a seatbelt. He reaches again, but this time for the key and the Mustang's 390-cubic-inch V-8 engine whinnies, fires, then settles to a throaty, throbbing burble. The *Bullitt* theme thumps out a steady baseline as the Mustang slithers backward into the parking lot and pulls away into the traffic. The Charger follows, the saxophones begin their famous riff. It's started.

It doesn't take a helluva lot to work out why *Bullitt* is still the greatest of them all. For the next few minutes the two deadly adversaries (and we are left with no doubt that this match will be deadly) play a low-key game of cat-and-mouse, the hunting Charger soon losing the Mustang in San Francisco's backstreets. But the hunter becomes the hunted as bad guy Phil (Bill Hickman) does a double take when he spots the Mustang in the rear-view mirror. The hit man has been wrong-footed already and is visibly shaken. He knows he's in trouble, we know he's in trouble, and from that moment the tension ratchets up a couple of notches. We, the audience, try to remain civilized, but that's just too tough to call. We bay for blood.

Close-ups of Phil's face, shot from a low camera angle in the car, cut to an in-car head and shoulders shot of Frank Bullitt. Director Peter Yates is giving us sight of the opponents once more before the battle starts in earnest. Then we're riding

Solar Productions/Warner Bros/RGA

with Bullitt, the Charger is in view, and the Mustang may as well be wearing a gun sight at the end of its long nose. Bullitt cruises close behind the Charger, a cable-car bell clangs, and the horn section of the band ups the tempo. Then that seminal moment arrives. Phil pulls up to a junction, stops, and the camera crops tight on his hands fastening the seat belt. He pulls a flanker by cruising gently away from the lights, then floors the throttle and swings violently left across the traffic. Bullitt is caught out, almost loses the plot, gets blocked by a cab, and rages with frustration. He flings the wheel around, finds a gap, and doesn't so much drive as unleash the mighty GT's 390 V-8 with a feral roar and howl of tires that makes your spine tingle. The race is on, and there can be only one winner.

It's not just the inclusion of the fabulous cars, the fabulous city, and the King of Cool that makes *Bullitt* the best chase in the world, although all three factors have got a lot to do with it. The engine soundtrack of both cars is simply awesome and watchable until the DVD player wears out. The cinematography broke new ground and the in-car footage is raw and gritty with plenty of opportunity to watch Hickman, McQueen, and Bud Ekins—and whomever else was driving the Mustang—in action. The chase is awash with inconsistencies. People often talk sneeringly about the number of hubcaps the Charger loses and the reappearing green VW Beetle. But who cares? The editing has a superb linearity and watching Hickman corner the huge Charger in full-blooded four-wheel drifts and the Mustang leaping the hills of San Francisco more than makes up for any continuity snags. There can be no doubt. *Bullitt* is a masterpiece of filmmaking.

INDEX